53
Interesting Ways
to Supervise Student
Projects, Dissertations
and Theses

For our students

53
Interesting Ways
to Supervise Student
Projects, Dissertations
and Theses

Vicky Lewis
Professor of Education, Open University

Sue Habeshaw
Senior Lecturer, Faculty of Humanities,
University of the West of England, Bristol

Technical and Educational Services Ltd
First published in 1997 by
Technical and Educational Services Ltd
37 Ravenswood Road
Bristol BS6 6BW
UK

ISBN 0 947885 92 7

Printed in Great Britain by The Cromwell Press, Melksham, Wiltshire

*TES Books are distributed by
Plymbridge Distributors Ltd.
Estover
Plymouth PL6 7PZ*

*For Customer Services
telephone +44 (0) 1752 202301 or fax orders +44 (0) 1752 202333*

Books from Technical & Educational Services

The 53 series
53 Interesting Things to Do in Your Lectures
53 Interesting Things to Do in Your Seminars and Tutorials
53 Interesting Ways to Assess Your Students
53 Interesting Ways of Helping Your Students to Study
53 Interesting Communication Exercises for Science Students
53 Interesting Ways to Appraise Your Teaching
53 Interesting Ways to Teach Mathematics
53 Problems with Large Classes: *Making the Best of a Bad Job*
53 Interesting Ways to Write Open Learning Materials
53 Interesting Activities for Open Learning Courses
53 Interesting Ways to Promote Equal Opportunities in Education
53 Questions and Answers about Semesters and Modules

Interesting ways to teach
Preparing to Teach: An Introduction to Effective Teaching in Higher
     Education
253 Ideas for Your Teaching
Interesting Ways to Teach: 12 Do-It-Yourself Staff Development
     Exercises

Other titles
Getting the Most from Your Data: Practical Ideas on how to Analyse
     Qualitative Data
Writing Study Guides
Improving the Quality of Student Learning
Teaching University Students Chemistry
Essential Chemistry for Advanced Biologists
HMA Stationery Ltd

About the authors

Vicky Lewis is Professor of Education and Director of the Centre for Human Development and Learning in the School of Education at the Open University. She is a developmental psychologist and has had the experience of being supervised, obtaining a DPhil from Oxford University in 1976.
She has successfully supervised MSc and PhD research students as well as numerous final year undergraduate projects. She runs workshops nationally on 'Supervising research students' and 'Succeeding as a research student' for supervisors and students respectively.

Sue Habeshaw is Senior Lecturer and Course Advisor in the Faculty of Humanities at the University of the West of England. She teaches literature, drama, study skills and various aspects of personal development including co-counselling and assertiveness. She is co-author of nine books in the series *Interesting Ways to Teach*. She has a lot of experience of running workshops for supervisors and supervisees.

Contents   Page

When things go wrong

Acknowledgements

We would like to thank the following people for their help and support.

Glyn Collis
George Dunbar
Adele Graham
Trevor Habeshaw
Eira Makepeace

Introduction

The need for this book arises from the general lack of provision of supervision training in higher education: even those institutions which mount teaching courses for new staff tend not to include in their programmes any training in the role of supervisor as this is a position which people usually only graduate to after some time in the job. This means that many people find themselves supervising dissertation or research students without any kind of advice or training. At best they may try to learn from the practice of their own supervisors; at worst they may uncritically replicate the supervision they themselves received. Because supervision is normally one-to-one, the dissemination of new and interesting ways of doing things - or even regular ways of doing things - is restricted.

With this in mind, we have written a book which is addressed to both new and established supervisors and covers both standard practice and new ideas. Because of our own experiences as supervisors in the arts, humanities and social sciences, many ideas originate in these areas. However, we hope that they will also be useful to supervisors working in other areas.

The fifty-three items in this book are written to be freestanding suggestions but they are collected into cognate chapters and cross-referenced where this may be helpful. Some of the items are broad-based and others are more specific. Most of them relate equally to undergraduate and postgraduate students; where an item relates specifically to one group or the other, this is made clear in the item's title.

It is a characteristic of this book that it features individual students and supervisors and therefore makes frequent use of the singular personal pronoun. Rather than keep repeating the phrase 'he or she' or 'she or he' we have decided, as women supervisors ourselves, to refer to the supervisor as 'she' and the student as 'he'.

We hope that you and your students will be able to benefit from this book to build supervision relationships which are honest, supportive, enjoyable and productive.

Preparing to supervise

1 Developing your skills
2 Matching undergraduate students with supervisors
3 Recruiting research students
4 Supporting postgraduate students from overseas
5 Which research degree?

Developing your skills 1

In higher education it is often assumed that anybody with a particular qualification is competent to supervise students who are working for that qualification. While this is an obvious prerequisite, the skills of a supervisor are clearly different from those of a student (and from those of a lecturer) and need to be developed. Here are some ways in which you can develop your skills.

- **Learning the rules**
  Find out what regulations and guidelines are produced for supervisors and students by your institution, department and any relevant funding body or professional organisation. Familiarise yourself with them and make sure that your students know about them. If you spot any gaps in the information, ask your colleagues what the departmental procedure is. If they are unclear, suggest that the issue is put on the agenda for discussion at the next departmental meeting.

- **Sitting by Nellie**
  'Sitting by Nellie' is a term which refers to the situation in which the inexperienced worker sits in with the experienced worker, observes what she does and tries to learn from it. Pairs of supervisors who set this up (with the permission of the student, of course) and discuss the tutorials afterwards find that they both benefit from the experience. In fact some institutions insist that inexperienced supervisors always supervise students jointly with an experienced supervisor.

- **Training**
  If you feel, as an inexperienced or experienced supervisor, that you need practical training, it is important that you ask for it. Workshops on supervising students are available nationally or can be provided specifically for your institution or department if there is sufficient demand[1].

- **Looking at existing theses**

  The best way of keeping up to date with standards and developments and possibilities in your area is to look at existing theses. Some of these will be available in your institution's own library; others can be ordered through inter-library loan. It is also a good idea to track down any theses in your department which are of special note, because the work was thought to be either outstanding or inadequate or controversial; if possible talk to the tutor concerned about the experience of supervising that student.

- **Putting yourself in the student's place**

  Empathy is probably the most important skill of any supervisor. You can empathise with your students if you put their needs first, remember in general terms what it was like to be a student yourself and try to imagine in particular what it is like to be these students. (If you find this difficult, you could try role playing the part of one of your students with a colleague.) If you are able to see the process from your students' points of view, you won't go far wrong.

- **Learning from feedback**

  Ask your students for feedback. Listen carefully to what they say and amend your practice if appropriate.

- **Learning through examining**

  As an internal or external examiner you can develop your skills by comparing your colleagues' assessment criteria, judgments and decisions with your own. In particular, discussions between first and second markers, and between internal and external examiners, provide a rich basis for the development of skills.

[1] For further information ring the Oxford Centre for Staff & Learning Development on 01 865 484610 at Oxford Brookes University, Oxford OX3 0P, UK.

Matching undergraduate students with supervisors 2

Students on undergraduate degrees who are required to produce a dissertation or carry out a project are generally expected to be responsible for choosing their own topic and carrying out the necessary research. They do, however, need to be able to seek advice from a member of staff. This advice may include helping the student to select a suitable topic, suggesting appropriate materials to consult, assisting with the design of an empirical study, advising on data analysis and reading drafts of the dissertation or project. For such supervision to be effective it is important that ways are set up to link particular students with particular members of staff. Several ways in which this matching can be facilitated are suggested below.

* **Staff interest list**
  Ask all members of staff to produce a list of areas in which they would be interested to supervise undergraduate dissertations or projects. It is useful to identify two sorts of area. The first should be very general topic areas, such as Child Psychology or European Literature. The second should be much more specific topic areas within each general area. Thus for Child Psychology these might include children's drawings, children's development of theory of mind, pretend play, whereas for European Literature possible topics might be Expressionism, Surrealism, Existentialism, Modernism, Postmodernism. As a department you might also decide that you want to include some very specific project or dissertation topics. However if you do this you will need to discuss the implications for assessment of having some ideas originating from students and some from staff (for a suggestion on how this might be done see item 43, *Second marking procedure for undergraduate projects and dissertations*).

  The list should give the names of all members of staff and information on how they can be contacted such as their room number, telephone extension, email address. Then their general area(s) of interest should be listed followed by their more narrow topic areas. The list should either be posted on an appropriate noticeboard or, and this is preferable, produced as a handout and given to every student.

The availability of such a list has a number of advantages. In addition to enabling students to seek a supervisor with appropriate interests, it will help those students who cannot think of a suitable topic but know they are interested in a particular area to identify which member of staff to approach. It will also provide students who cannot think of a topic with an idea of the range of topics which are feasible.

- **Appoint a project/dissertation course leader**
  The role of the project/dissertation course leader is to have an initial discussion with each student and to explore the student's areas of interest in order to identify a suitable supervisor. Once a member of staff has been identified the student contacts her to discuss the idea further.

This approach has several advantages over producing a staff interest list (though in a large department it may be useful also to produce a list so that the course leader and the students have up to date information on staff interests). One advantage of appointing a course leader is that one member of staff is responsible for matching students with staff and can therefore try to ensure that staff supervise roughly equivalent numbers of students. A second advantage is that before embarking on the project or dissertation all students will have the opportunity to discuss the scope of the piece of work with the same member of staff. This will help ensure that the amount of work carried out by different students will be roughly equivalent, something which is more difficult to control if different staff are supervising different students from the outset, unless clear guidelines have been discussed and agreed. Obviously the main disadvantage to this approach, especially in a large department, is the amount of time required for one member of staff to see all students.

• **Project/dissertation outline**
Students hand in an outline of the topic they are interested in studying for their project or dissertation. Ideally this should identify a particular area of interest and, if possible, the research question they want to consider. The outline should provide some justification for the research and an indication of how the research will be carried out (for an empirical study this might include the design of the project, the participants to be involved, some indication of the data to be collected and how it will be analysed; for a dissertation the outline might include the scope of the topic, the approach to be taken and the sources to be considered).

The outlines are circulated among staff who identify those projects or dissertations they would be willing to supervise, in order of preference. The dissertation course leader then allocates students to supervisors, bearing in mind staff preferences and balance of workload.

• **Combination of approaches**
Rather than using one of the above suggestions in isolation it may be best to match students with supervisors by combining the ideas. One possible combination would be as follows. Initially a staff interest list is produced and circulated to all students. Students then have an appointment with the project/dissertation course leader who gives them general guidance on what is expected and feasible and suggests an appropriate supervisor. The students meet with their supervisors and, following discussion, produce a project/dissertation outline which is handed in and seen by the course leader and the individual supervisor. If the outline is approved the supervisor contacts the student to arrange to meet to discuss the next step. If the outline is not approved the supervisor arranges to see the student to discuss how the proposal needs to change. Following this the student puts in a revised outline which is considered again. It is important that deadlines for each stage are set out and made clear to the students. These could be

19

included with the initial circulation of the staff interest list, along with general guidelines about the project/dissertation.

Recruiting research students 3

Postgraduate research students can contribute a great deal: they are usually keen and excited about their research and may have innovative ideas and suggestions for research which will make them valued colleagues; they can help establish a research culture and improve the research standing of a department or school; they may also contribute to undergraduate teaching and the general social life of the department. However, in the present financial climate, it is becoming increasingly difficult for such students to obtain funding.

If you want to increase the number of funded research students at your institution, you will need to be strategic. There are several things you can do. These are listed below.

- **Appoint a Director of Postgraduate Studies**
  This will give status to the position of postgraduate study in your department. This is important as a marketing strategy. Students are likely to be deterred from applying to your department if, following their initial enquiry, they are passed from person to person without anyone having specific responsibility for them. If on the other hand one person coordinates everything to do with postgraduate study, this will give a good impression. Obviously the person appointed will need to be committed to the development of postgraduate research and be experienced in supervising postgraduates.

- **Obtain funding for postgraduates**
  Be pro-active. In order to optimise the likelihood of obtaining funding it is crucial that you make yourself familiar with funding availability and criteria for applying produced by funding councils, charities and any other relevant organisations.

- **Publicise opportunities for postgraduate study**
  You cannot expect people outside your department to realise that you

are willing to supervise postgraduates unless you tell them. One way to do this is to produce a flier outlining the possibilities and send it to relevant departments in other institutions with a request that it be displayed on an appropriate noticeboard. A flier successfully used by Vicky Lewis is reproduced at the end of this item.

If you obtain funding for a research student, advertise the position in the national press and on electronic mailing systems as well as circulating information around relevant departments. Although such advertising will be orientated to the specific studentship, the advertising itself will raise awareness of the opportunities for postgraduate study in your department.

- **Establish your reputation**
  If students are interested in pursuing research in particular areas they are likely to seek out and read the available literature and discuss possible departments with their tutors. Obviously if you have published in their area of interest this will increase the likelihood that they will approach your department about postgraduate possibilities. However it is also important that staff in other institutions are made aware of postgraduate opportunities in your department. You can do this by circulating a flier and also by attending relevant conferences. In particular, if you have current research students, encourage them to present papers and present papers yourself. If you and your students contribute regularly at conferences, word will soon get around that your department has an active group of postgraduates with supporting staff. This will encourage applications.

University of Warwick
School of Graduate Studies & Department of Psychology
Postgraduate Research in Developmental Psychology

> **Topics in Developmental Psychology currently being investigated at Warwick include:**
> autism and other developmental disorders
> symbolic play
> children's theories of mind
> children's drawings
> semantic development
> adult-child communication
> visual impairment
> lateralisation in developmentally disordered children

The Developmental Psychology group at Warwick is led by Vicky Lewis and Glyn Collis who are in close contact with developmental and clinical psychologists in the University's Department of Education and School of Postgraduate Medical Education. Good working relations have been established with schools, playgroups, maternity hospitals etc.

Most students are supervised jointly by Drs Lewis and Collis. In addition to individual supervision, the whole group meets regularly to discuss current progress, shared interests and wider issues in Developmental Psychology.

Work with children with disordered development is encouraged. However, potential applicants should be aware that, in many cases, it is advisable to start a programme of research with empirical work on normal children.

Applications are invited from suitably qualified persons for the research degrees of MSc (1 year) MPhil (2 years) or PhD (3 years). Students wishing to read for the degree of PhD are normally required to register in the first instance for the degree of MPhil; transfer to registration for a PhD will be permitted for students showing aptitude and making good progress in their research and written reports. In exceptional cases, research degrees may be available on a part-time basis.

The department is recognised as an outlet for ESRC studentships.

Informal enquiries may be made to:
Dr Glyn Collis (tel 01203 523182)   **Dr Vicky Lewis (tel 01203 523158)**
Department of Psychology   Department of Psychology
University of Warwick   University of Warwick
Coventry CV4 7AL   Coventry CV4 7AL
or to the Director of Postgraduate Studies, Department of Psychology.
Completed application forms should be sent to the Registry.

Supporting postgraduate students from overseas 4

Many universities are keen to recruit students from overseas. This may be because they hope to enrich the experience of staff and students through international contact, or because they want to increase research student numbers and foreign governments will often fund such students to study in the UK. When institutions decide to take on overseas students, they may overlook the need for extra support - and hence in fact extra time and extra funding - that responsibility for these students entails.

If you are called on to supervise overseas students, you will probably find that they need more support than your home students, particularly if this is their first experience of studying abroad. If English is not their first language you will need to allow them more time for their reading and writing and offer them more thorough discussion of their ideas and detailed editing of their drafts than you would in the case of native speakers of English. For this reason you may want to try to negotiate yourself an extra time allowance for such supervision.

If you are supervising research students from overseas you should find the following recommendations helpful. They are points from *The Management of Higher Degrees Undertaken by Overseas Students*, a paper produced for universities in 1992 by the Committee of Vice Chancellors and Principals. The full version of the paper should be available in your institution.

* *Universities are strongly advised to establish a student's English language competence before arrival in the UK. Where a university decides to admit a student despite the lack of a satisfactory knowledge of English, it should ensure that the student is provided with language tuition at the expense of the institution.*

* *Progress reports to the sponsoring authority should be made at least annually.*

- *Students should be encouraged to draw any problems to the attention of the university as soon as these occur.*

- *Academic supervisors should be particularly sensitive to the needs of overseas students who may need more supervision time than others. Universities should ensure that guidance on this matter is offered to supervisors.*

- *Supervisors should be realistic in their assessment of the time likely to be required for the completion of a course.*

Which research degree? 5

In order to be eligible for research studentships funded by research councils it is normally necessary for departments to be able to demonstrate that a substantial proportion of those students who are registered for PhDs submit their theses within the appropriate time limit. Such performance indicators are also important for persuading other agencies, such as charities, to provide funding. This means that it is essential to admit only those students who are highly likely to complete on time. In reality this is essentially impossible since, as a potential supervisor, the only information likely to be available to you about a student is his research proposal, two or three academic references and the outcome of an interview.

One solution to this problem is initially to admit all research students to an MPhil rather than to a PhD. Similarly, students who wish to register for an MPhil can be admitted to an MSc or MA by research.

For example, in the case of a two-year MPhil/three-year PhD arrangement, this would give the department the opportunity to monitor the student's progress carefully over the course of the first year (see item 35, *Records and reports*) and towards the end of the year consider a recommendation for upgrade to a PhD (see item 36, *Postgraduate Supervisory Committee*). If, at the end of the first year, it was not felt that the student's progress warranted upgrade, he could be encouraged to complete an MPhil or alternatively to make more progress with a view to the possibility of an upgrade being considered in several months' time.

Such an arrangement can also be seen as beneficial for students. A student who has completed a first degree will have had little experience of sustained research and may be grateful for the opportunity of completing an MPhil rather than struggling on with a PhD. In the case of students from overseas who may arrive with very different undergraduate experience this arrangement gives the department the opportunity to assess the likelihood that the students will be able to manage a PhD.

Establishing relationships

Questions to ask undergraduate students 6

Students are individuals: they have different aims, different needs and different ways of working. In order to be able to offer the most appropriate supervision to each individual student, you will need to put questions to each one about his needs and preferences. Key questions relate to the students' purpose, their view of the supervisor's role and their preferences for the timing of the meetings. (See also item 8, *Arranging meetings*.)

Before they can answer such questions fully, however, students need time to reflect on the issues and consider their replies. It is helpful, therefore, if you give them the questions first in written form with a brief explanation of what you intend by each one.

A sample set of questions is given below. If you use this list you will want to amend it to suit your own situation.

After giving students your questions to answer, you can begin the following supervision tutorial by discussing their answers with them individually and pressing them to be really explicit about their aims, needs and ways of working.

Questions for dissertation students
Please give some time to considering these questions. We will discuss your answers at the next supervision tutorial.

- **What is your purpose?**
  Some students want to do a dissertation/project for its own sake and for their personal development and they don't care much what the examiners think. Other students want to score as many marks as possible and want advice on how to do this. You can adopt either position or a compromise between the two. I don't mind which you choose but you do need to be aware of your purpose because other decisions depend on it.

- **What would you like my role to be?**
  I would like to help you in whatever way is best for you. You are the only real judge of this. So I would like you to think about this so that you can be clear about what you want from me. I would also like you to give me feedback as we go along so that I know if I'm doing it right or not.

- **How would you like to distribute your time allowance?**
  Supervisors have a time allowance of 'x' minutes per student per week. So you can have a tutorial of that length every week, or twice that length every fortnight etc. (It's OK for this to be different at different times of the year.)

Questions to ask postgraduate students 7

There are many differences between being an undergraduate student and being a postgraduate student, especially if the postgraduate degree is examined solely by a thesis. Undergraduates are normally provided with a timetable and reading lists and expected to produce written work and take exams at particular points in the year. Postgraduate research students will be assigned to a supervisor and will know that they have one, two or three years, or maybe more if registered part-time, in which to produce a thesis. General guidelines may be produced by the institution or department concerning issues such as the expected frequency of supervisions, the characteristics of different research degrees, and the nature of the final examination. However, newly arrived postgraduates will not have a clear idea of what is expected of them, what they can expect of their supervisor, the department or the institution. Also since supervisors differ in how they approach the process of supervising students it is important that very early on you clarify your approach (see also item 9, *Personal style*).

One way to do this is to use questions to prompt discussion of what you expect of research students and what they can expect from you, the department and the institution. Adele Graham from the Higher Education Research Office at Auckland University in New Zealand has produced a useful set of questions which can be used in this way. These are reproduced following this item. When you have looked at these guidelines, you may decide to produce your own list of questions to use with postgraduates.

When new postgraduates arrive give them a copy of Adele Graham's guidelines, or your own version, and suggest that they look through the questions carefully and note any additional ones they think of. Ensure that they also have copies of any general information produced by the department and the institution. Arrange to meet with them a few days later specifically to go through the guidelines. When you meet, go through each question in turn, describing honestly your view of the situation and seeking their comments. Allow plenty of time for this meeting as the discussion will be very important in establishing your relationship with the students, in particular clarifying what you expect of them and what they can expect of you.

University of Auckland
Postgraduate Supervision
Guidelines for discussion

Adele Graham (HERO) & Barbara Grant (SLC & HERO)

Introduction

This booklet is designed to be used in an early discussion between supervisor and postgraduate student. It is based on our assumption that there are some basic issues which underpin effective supervision and we believe that by discussing these issues the foundations are laid for a good working relationship. Different aspects may need to be renegotiated during the process.

In preparing this booklet we envisaged that both student and supervisor would respond to the issues below. One of the main objectives of this process is to share understandings so that there is agreement over fundamental (and often mistakenly assumed) beliefs and expectations. You will notice that space has been left for one of you to record your joint understandings. We suggest a copy is made of the completed document for each party.

We have put personal issues first because they are most immediate to the supervision process and then listed departmental and university-level issues that are also relevant.

Important note: If there are *two or more supervisors*, we suggest that this document be negotiated amongst all parties.

We would like to thank those postgraduate students and staff members of the University of Auckland who gave us helpful feedback in the shaping of this booklet.

Adele Graham/Barbara Grant   April 1993

Name of student: _____

Name(s) or supervisor(s): _____

_____

Date: _____

Supervisor/Student Understandings

1 What is a thesis?

- what does 'thesis' mean?
- what form should a thesis proposal have?
- what is the appropriate structure of a thesis?
- what is the appropriate length?
- what referencing conventions should I follow?
- what is the difference between a thesis that passes and one that is first class?
- some titles of good thesis examples in this field?
- what is meant by 'originality'?
- who owns papers arising during and after thesis supervision?

2 Meetings

- frequency and duration of meetings?
- access to supervisor outside of scheduled meeting times?
- who has responsibility to initiate meetings (if not scheduled regularly)?
- protocol for when one person can't make the meeting?

3 Advice and support

- development of the research proposal: how much input from supervisor? how will this proceed?
- expectations of feedback: how much, how often, in what form, with how much notice?
- support with theoretical content, e.g. resources, contacts: how much can be expected, given the supervisor's knowledge of the area?
- what other kinds of knowledge are needed, e.g. of the research process, of academic writing etc. - what resources does the supervisor know of? how much help can s/he give?

- are there relevant personal circumstances that might make the supervision or completion of the thesis difficult, e.g. student suffering financial hardship or experiencing relationship difficulties or supervisor going on sabbatical, expecting a baby or ...?

4 Time frame

- how long should the different stages take to complete?
- what would be a realistic completion date in view of our separate commitments and departmental policy?

5 Joint supervisors

- what roles will be taken by each supervisor, e.g. main and secondary, different theoretical inputs?
- if there is disagreement about methods etc. between joint supervisors, how is this to be resolved?

6 Other issues relating to supervisor/student understandings?

Departmental expectations and resources

1 Written information

- what departmental handbooks or other documents are relevant for postgraduate students?

2 What access does the student have to

- a study place, pigeon hole etc?
- tea/coffee facilities?
- photocopying, interloan fees etc?
- paid work, e.g. tutoring?

- computer?
- funding/research grants?
  If available how do I apply? When are the deadlines? Who can I contact for more information?
- support services, e.g. technical, secretarial?

3 What expectations does the department have of the student?

- seminar presentation of thesis in progress?
- what else?

4 Monitoring supervision, resolving conflict

What are the departmental procedures for monitoring the supervsion in the event that one of us is not happy with its progress?

5 Other departmental issues?

University requirements

1 University guidelines

What University documents are available on Masters level supervision? e.g. the University of Auckland 1992 guidelines, *Supervision of Theses and Dissertations at Masters Level.*

2 Clarification of thesis assessment

- how is the assessment of the thesis conducted?
- who will be the external examiner? When is this decided? Can the student have a say?

3 Extensions and deferment

- what are the protocols for extensions and deferment?
- in the event that I need an extension over the summer, or beyond, what will the position be regarding supervision?

4 University protocols

What university-level channels are available in the event that one of us is not happy with the progress of the supervision and the department cannot or is inappropriate to resolve this?

5 Ethics

- what ethical issues need to be considered in the research project?
- do I need to apply for consent from an appropriate university committee?

6 Other university-level issues?

Arranging meetings 8

One of the aims of education must be to produce independent learners. Yet a great deal of education provides minimal opportunity for independence to develop. Even in higher education students will be told what they should be reading, which lectures they should attend and so on. However one way in which independence can be developed is through the use of projects, dissertations and theses. Here students are able to take a certain amount of responsibility for what they do and how they do it, but with the support of a supervisor who can advise. In order for this to work effectively it is important that as the supervisor you think carefully about how much support you provide - and when - and convey this to your student.

When students are embarking on a piece of research, whether for a project, dissertation or thesis, it may be necessary for you to offer them frequent meetings. At this stage when they are working out what to do and how to go about it they may need to see you every day for several days in a row, or even several times a day. Each time they may have moved on very little and the meetings may be very short. Nevertheless such meetings are important and will help them gain the confidence to take bigger steps without your support.

It is useful to explain when you start supervising that the intervals between meetings, the lengths of the meetings and the content of your discussions will vary over their total period of study. Point out that in the early stages you will probably meet more frequently than later on. Stress however that they can ask for a meeting when they feel that one would be useful. It is also important to set a maximum interval between meetings which will depend on the length of the period of study involved. For example, with a PhD student, it would be reasonable to see the student at least once every six weeks, with the expectation that over the course of three years, meetings would average out to one meeting lasting an hour per fortnight.

The focus of your meetings will also vary over time. It will range from early supervisions in which possible questions and issues are considered, through discussion of relevant literature and approaches, to consideration of the student's own contribution to the area, with later supervisions examining drafts of parts of the project, dissertation or thesis.

Personal style 9

Personal style is fundamental to the supervision relationship. All tutors have their personal style, which depends on their personality, experience and perception of their role. Some tutors believe that it is more professional to have a formal style while others prefer to have an informal working relationship with students. For example, some will address their student as Mr Smith and expect to be called Professor Lewis; others will be happy with the names John and Vicky. Some will prefer to hold tutorials in their offices; others will suggest meeting in the refectory or bar. Some will exchange home phone numbers with their students; others will prefer to maintain a boundary between their professional and private lives.

While there are dangers of taking these to extremes so that either the supervisor intimidates the student or is afraid to offer any criticisms, it is advisable to adopt the style which you feel most comfortable with. That way you will be more true to yourself and come across as genuine.

Students have a personal style too. Some may prefer to have a close relationship with their tutors while others prefer to be more distant. They will normally however take the lead from their supervisor.

It is important to be aware of your personal style and to ensure that your students are aware of it too. If there is a clash of expectations between you and your students, you will need to talk it through with them and negotiate a way of working which you both feel comfortable with. (See also item 7, *Questions to ask postgraduate students.*)

Sharing   **10**

As a supervisor you have more experience than the students you are supervising. It is very likely that you will have an equivalent qualification to the one your students are seeking and you may have additional qualifications. These qualifications, as well as your position in the institution, will set you apart from your students. In particular they will see you as someone who has succeeded, which may be very different from the way in which they see themselves. At times they may feel they are struggling and are not up to the demands placed on them. This can be especially true of project, dissertation or thesis work where students are expected to be more self sufficient.

One way in which you as a supervisor can help to develop a productive and supportive relationship with your students is by being open with them about how you feel about your role and your expertise and, more importantly, any lack of expertise you feel. It may also be the case that your progression to the position you now hold was not easy: at times you may have felt that you were not up to what was expected of you; you may have experienced particular problems at certain stages; you may still have difficulties with certain aspects of your work. It can be very useful to share some of these experiences with your students. It can help them to realise that many students, even those who go on to be successful, experience difficulties and have to overcome them. It should also help establish a good honest relationship between you and your students in which they can discuss the difficulties they are experiencing without feeling totally inferior.

While sharing your experiences with your students can be very useful it is important to remember that the focus should be on helping your students rather than vice versa: sharing your experiences should serve the purpose of encouraging your students to feel able to discuss any difficulties with you and it should not turn into a counselling session for you.

Cultural differences 11

It is easy for two people from different cultures to misunderstand each other. This is even easier if one is a teacher who is wary of being racist and the other is a student who has been taught never to question authority: two people like this could work together for years without ever recognising their cultural differences.

Some cultural differences like accent, clothing and the keeping of religious and national holidays, are obvious. Others, like the cultural rules governing eye contact or a preference for which part of a person's name should be used to address him or her, are less obvious. Others again are fundamental to the supervision relationship. For example, students from other cultures may find it difficult to be taught by a woman; they may have so much respect for their teachers that they consider it disrespectful to ask questions; or they may have been educated in a system where the teacher is the only authority and students expect to be told what to learn.

The situation is complicated by the fact that many students whose physical appearance might lead you to expect that they would be culturally different have in fact been born and educated in Britain and see themselves as culturally British.

The only way to deal with the potential difficulties of cultural differences is to be direct and honest: it is not racist to ask questions about an individual's background when it is your intention to be helpful. Ask your students to describe their educational histories and assumptions. If they have roots in another culture, try to find out to what extent they want to keep to their own ways of doing things and to what extent they want to adopt British ways. Try to negotiate a working arrangement that you and they can be happy with: your aim should be to respect difference while trying to help students to be successful in the British system.

(See also item 4, *Supporting postgraduate students from overseas*.)

Getting students started

Helping undergraduate students to choose a topic 12

Many undergraduate students have no ideas about a suitable question on which to base their dissertation or project. Even students who have identified a topic may need help in specifying the precise question to be addressed. As a supervisor there are several ways in which you can help your students to do this. The suggestion below takes the form of a series of four meetings, with the student preparing material for each meeting, which culminate in an agreed proposal. You will need to adapt the nature and number of the meetings to suit the individual needs of particular students. You will also need to consider the timing of the meetings bearing in mind the total time available. You may also want to introduce a deadline for the handing in of a final proposal (see Meeting 4).

Meeting 1: Asking questions

Assuming that a student has chosen you as a supervisor because you have an interest in a particular area (see item 2, *Matching undergraduate students with supervisors*), you can help him identify a suitable topic by asking a series of open-ended questions. Possible questions might be: 'What aspects of [the general area] have you found particularly interesting?' 'What was it about these that interested you?' 'Did you find yourself wanting to ask further questions about [the area of interest] which were not addressed in what you read?' 'What would you really like to know about [the area of interest]?'

Preparatory work for Meeting 2: Searching the literature

Once students have identified a topic, suggest that they look at what has been written on it. They are unlikely to be able to read everything on a given topic so suggest that they start with recent publications, perhaps beginning with a literature search (see item 14, *Skills students need*). You will need to give them guidance on how to focus their reading. This will vary depending on whether a dissertation or practical project is being produced, although both sets of students will need to read critically. Project students need to ask questions to enable them to identify a project topic. Useful questions are those which ask whether the results of a particular study could be interpreted in a different way (this might lead to a study testing the alternative interpretations) or whether the results could be extended in any way. Dissertation students need to focus on the range of approaches to their topic and the variety of interpretations and responses.

For the second meeting students should prepare a written list of possible research questions (for projects) or different approaches and interpretations (for dissertations).

Meeting 2: Exploring possibilities
This meeting should focus on the ideas that the student has identified from the literature search, with the aim of selecting a specific research question or approach/interpretation to focus on. You need to guide the student to something which is realistic in terms of the time and, for project work, the resources available.

Preparatory work for Meeting 3: Specifying the topic
For the next meeting students should prepare written details of what they are planning to do: project students should specify the design of their study and dissertation students should clarify the approaches/interpretations to be covered.

Meeting 3: Agreeing the topic
This meeting is to consider the students' written plans. As the supervisor you may need to give them suggestions about ways in which they need to alter their proposals.

Preparatory work for Meeting 4: Drafting a proposal
The student should now be in a position to draft an outline proposal. The draft proposal should follow the different phases of the final report: a project proposal should give the background to the project, the method, an indication of the analyses to be carried out, and possible interpretation of

the results; the dissertation proposal could be a set of chapter headings and summaries.

Meeting 4: Agreeing the proposal

At this meeting any changes to the student's proposal should be agreed. The student should now be in a position to embark on his project or dissertation.

Helping postgraduate students to refine a research question   13

Postgraduate students need to identify a suitable research question before they can embark on any research. This can be a daunting task because as undergraduates they may have had little or no experience of the way in which research arises, how research questions are chosen or how they relate to existing literature in the area: the majority of their experience will have come either from reading published accounts of research, or from carrying out projects based on ideas or questions suggested by lecturers.

You need to explain to your students that new research normally relates quite closely to existing literature, in one of two ways. It may examine alternative explanations for particular observations other than those offered (and ways of testing these alternatives) or it may consider questions arising from existing research findings but not answered by them. Provided that your students know which general area they want to work in, encourage them to identify and critically read relevant material bearing in mind that they are looking for alternative explanations or unanswered questions.

Students may need help in thinking about how to organise material in ways that will enable them to identify a research question. They may find it useful to organise their material visually (see 'Pictures' in item 18, *Helping students to organise information*). Presenting material in this way makes it much easier to see gaps or controversies in the literature as well as connections between different areas. These visual plans may also be useful to them when they come to write up their theses, so they should be encouraged to keep them (see item 15, *Basic advice for students*).

Skills students need 14

It is very easy to assume that when students reach the stage of carrying out a research project or writing a dissertation they will have already acquired the skills they need. These include using an on-line library catalogue, carrying out an on-line literature search, analysing data, structuring a dissertation or project report, and word processing. Postgraduate students may also find it useful to be able to network with students in other institutions working in similar areas either via electronic mail user groups or via the Internet (see item 41, *Supervising postgraduate students at a distance*).

Very often students manage to get by without acquiring all of these skills. If they leave it too long they may find it difficult simply because they assume that they should have already developed all the necessary skills. As a supervisor it is important that you identify the sorts of skills which your students should develop in order to complete their work as efficiently and competently as possible. You will then need to check with them whether or not there are particular skills which they lack and either teach them yourself or direct them to an appropriate source of help. Use the following checklist and suggestions for support to guide your discussions with students. Add any additional skills you feel are important.

Checklist of useful skills

* **On-line library catalogue**
  Many libraries now use an on-line cataloguing system which enables readers to check library holdings in a particular area, to find out whether a particular book is available, to reserve books and so on. These systems save a great deal of time otherwise spent physically searching the shelves and can be accessed from places outside the library if the system is networked.

  Make sure you know the arrangements that your library staff make for showing students how to use the catalogue.

- **On-line literature databases**
  In all areas of academic study there are nationally available on-line databases which can be used to find up-to-date literature on any specified topic. These databases are an invaluable resource for both students and supervisors, enabling very fast searches for relevant literature. However in many cases you need to register to get a password to allow you to access these systems.

  Familiarise yourself with the arrangements for using the databases relevant to your subject area and make use of them yourself. Also check if your library provides information and guidance on how to use these systems which you can pass on to students as necessary.

- **Data analysis**
  By the time that students have reached the stage of carrying out a research project they should have received training in the sorts of data analysis required. However some students may still have difficulties relating the procedures covered in that course to their own project.

  It is useful to get students to think about how they will analyse their data before they actually undertake any data collection. Such an exercise often leads to changes in the design of the study. Make sure you are familiar with appropriate statistical procedures and the packages available to run them. Find out which of your colleagues are available to offer statistical advice to students.

- **Structuring**
  One of the skills of producing a high quality project or dissertation involves following various guidelines on how to write it up. Most students are provided with such guidelines when they begin their period of study, especially for project reports. Nevertheless it is worth reminding them that the structure of the end product is important and that they should have this in mind throughout.

In addition to any departmental materials on writing up projects or dissertations, you can support the importance of structure in two ways. One is to refer students to published books, or chapters in books, which provide guidelines (see list of suggestions below). A second is to show them the completed projects or dissertations of previous students, obviously selecting work of a reasonably high standard. The latter may be particularly helpful to students embarking on a degree relying entirely on a research project or dissertation. However beware that this may produce worries of the sort 'I could never produce anything like that' and be prepared to reassure your students.

- **Word processing**
  Increasingly students are arriving at college or university with well developed word processing skills. Nevertheless don't assume that all your students will have the necessary skills or are familiar with the packages available. Also some students may appear to have good word processing skills but not make full use of the facilities. For example some may simply use a computer to type up the final report or dissertation and so miss the benefit of drafting directly onto the computer, with all the opportunities for easy editing that affords.

Check the provision available in your department for developing word processing and, if necessary, provide guidance yourself.

Phillips, E.M. & Pugh, D.S. (1994) *How to get a PhD: A handbook for students and their supervisors.* 2nd edn. Buckingham: Open University Press

Cryer, P. (1996) *The research student's guide to success.* Buckingham: Open University Press

Fairbairn, G.J. and Winch, C. (1996) *Reading, writing and reasoning: A guide for students.* 2nd edn. Buckingham: Open University Press

Bell, J. (1993) *Doing your research project: A guide for first-time researchers in education and social science.* Buckingham: Open University Press

Basic advice for students 15

When students embark on a project, dissertation or thesis their immediate focus is usually on their choice of topic and the process of carrying out the work rather than the final report. A consequence of this is that they may not consider how what they are doing at the early stages will relate to the later stage of writing up. As their supervisor it is important that you point out ways in which they may save themselves a great deal of time later on by getting into good habits from the beginning. You could devise a handout of tips which you give to your students or use the handout provided below.

Keeping a record

- **References**
  Keep a full record of every reference you read or consult. This record should have all the information needed to cite correctly the paper or book. You can either use separate file cards for each record and keep them safely or store the references on a computer (making sure you make a regular back-up copy).

- **Quotations**
  Keep the full reference of any quotation you write down, including the page number on which it occurs. It is also wise to take a photocopy of the quotation in order to check the wording and punctuation and, for books, the inside page showing the publisher, place of publication, date, edition, full title and author(s). This will ensure that you don't accidentally plagiarise.

- **Keep everything**
  Keep everything that you write. If you write summaries of what you are reading and what you think of it right from the beginning you may well find that you can incorporate bits of these summaries into your final report. The use of a wordprocessor will make the subsequent use of this material much easier.

- **Write up details at each stage**

  If the work involves an empirical study, it is essential that the procedural details are written up at the time of carrying out the research . Similarly you should keep a note of how you collate and analyse any results. At the time both of these may seem obvious, but important details may be overlooked if there is any delay in writing them down.

- **Make copies**

  As with references and written material it is important to make copies of any audio and video material if at all possible.

Contracts 16

The supervision relationship is one which is prone to all sorts of interpretations, assumptions and plain misunderstandings on both sides: supervisor and student may each imagine that it is the responsibility of the other to set the time scale, determine the reading list, proof read the drafts etc. Some students' - and supervisors' - understanding of supervision is that the tutor will make all the decisions and spoon-feed the student with information, advice and instructions. Others interpret the tutor's role as that of supporter and expect the student to take the initiative.

To prevent misunderstandings of this kind, student and supervisor need to compare their views and agree a description of their roles. This agreement can be drawn up as a formal contract.

If student and supervisor spend some time drawing up a contract which spells out the responsibilities of each role, things should run smoothly. If problems arise, either party can have recourse to the written agreement. An example of a contract follows.

A dissertation contract
- John is entitled to the equivalent of 15 minutes' supervision per week.
- If either John or Sue cannot keep an appointment, he or she will inform the other.
- John and Sue will negotiate the parameters of the dissertation.
- Sue will advise John on matters of feasibility and theoretical approaches.
- John is responsible for the literature search.
- Sue will give John written feedback on the first draft of each chapter.
- Sue will not read any drafts after the end of the spring term.
- John will be responsible for the proof reading.
- The dissertation is John's and he has final responsibility for it.

In addition, a project contract could include the following:

- Sue will point John towards relevant research papers.
- John will not carry out the project until it has been approved by Sue.
- John is responsible for ensuring that the project is ethical.
- John is responsible for making sure that any participants in the study are debriefed appropriately.
- Sue will give John written feedback on the first draft of the report.

Workshop on ethics   17

When students decide to embark on a research project, whether at under-graduate or postgraduate level, they often get carried away with their ideas and overlook the question of whether anyone else will be affected by their research. As a supervisor it is important that you consider the ethical issues of all research carried out by your students and if necessary submit the proposal to appropriate ethical committees for approval. It is also important that you raise your students' awareness of ethical issues which arise in research. One way of doing this is described below.

The length of time needed for this exercise will depend very much on how many students attend. With 10 students allow one and a half hours; for fewer than 10 students an hour will probably be sufficient; with more than 10 students allow two hours. The suggested timings given below assume a group of 12 students.

Before the meeting

a   Collect together any guidelines on ethical issues relevant to your discipline. These may include guidelines produced by your department, your institution or any professional bodies or research organisations who sponsor and oversee research in your area. Make enough copies for all students to have a set of the relevant documents or produce a summary paper of the main points yourself and photocopy it.

b   Find a day and time which are suitable for you and the students and book an appropriate room with chairs and tables which can be moved around and an overhead projector.

c   Circulate a note to all relevant students advertising the workshop. In the note ask the students to consider the following questions before the workshop and make brief notes on their answers:

Q1 Have any ethical issues arisen in your research so far? Describe.
Q2 What ethical issues do you think may arise in your research in the future? Describe.
Q3 Are there any general ethical issues which surround research in your discipline? Do these have any impact on your particular research project?

d   It is also useful if you find out from your colleagues whether there are particular ethical issues associated with their research. You could either do this informally or by asking them to provide written answers to the following sorts of questions:
Q1 What are the main ethical issues which arise in your area of research? Describe.
Q2 What ethical issues do you think may arise in your research in the future? Describe.
Q3 Are there any general ethical issues which surround research in your discipline? Do these have any impact on your area of research/current research project(s)?
Prepare a handout summarising the main ethical issues arising in your own and your colleagues' research.

At the meeting

Outline the purpose of the workshop as identifying ethical issues which arise in research and ways of ensuring that research projects take account of ethical guidelines. Explain that the first part of the workshop is concerned with identifying ethical issues which arise in research and the second part is to give the students the opportunity to consider the implications of relevant ethical guidelines for their own research projects.

Part 1
a   Check whether or not the students have done any preparation. If not give them 5 minutes to think about the questions previously circulated. Have further copies available for those who have forgotten theirs.

b   Ask the students to work in pairs and discuss their responses to the questions, identifying those ethical issues which are most relevant to them. Allow 10 minutes for this. At the end of this time and as a group ask each pair for the issues they have identified and list these (preferably on an OHP, leaving spaces for additional points to be added later). This will take a further 5 to 10 minutes.

c   Give out the summary of ethical issues identified by you and your colleagues which you have prepared. Ask the students in fours to consider the issues identified on the handout alongside the OHP list. Are the issues the same? Are there any differences? Can they see further issues which may arise in their own research in the future? Ask each group to make a list of any issues they would like to add to the original list. Allow a further 10 minutes for this.

d   Give out any guideline documents to each group of four students, providing if you can some general background to each set of guidelines. Ask each group of four to consider two questions:
    Q1 How do these guidelines relate to your own research?
    Q2 As a result of studying these guidelines can you identify further ethical issues which need to be added to our list?
    Each group should draw up a list of additions and amendments they would like to make to the original list of ethical issues displayed on the OHP. Allow 10 minutes for this.

e   The whole group should now consider the original list of issues arising from their research. Ask each group in turn to suggest an addition or amendment to the original list displayed on the OHP. Add these changes to the OHP using a differently coloured pen. Go around each group in turn until no more suggestions are forthcoming. This is likely to take at least 10 minutes.

Part 2
By this point in the workshop the group should have produced a fairly comprehensive list of ethical issues to be considered when carrying out

research. The aim of the second part of the workshop is for individual students to relate this list to their own research.

a   On their own all the students should take each point in turn and consider its relevance to their own research. For each point which is relevant they should briefly note down how they intend to meet the requirements of any guidelines. The length of time you allow for this part of the workshop will depend very much on the nature of the research being carried out. You will need to allow at least 10 minutes and possibly more if many issues have been identified.

b   When all the students have finished considering the implications for their research ask them to pair up and take 5 minutes to report to their partners how they intend to meet the guidelines. Each student should identify at least one issue and explain how he proposes meeting the relevant ethical guidelines.

c   In the final 10 minutes ask the students in turn in the whole group to tell the other students how they intend meeting a particular guideline.

After the meeting
Type up the amended OHP and circulate copies to all the students who attended the workshop.

Helping students to communicate

Helping students to organise information   18

Apart from what they write themselves students mainly read published papers and books. On the whole these will be fairly well written and will not convey what is involved in organising material prior to writing. Yet this organisation is a very important stage and is crucial to the clarity of the subsequent writing. You can help your students organise their own material by describing to them ways in which you organise material prior to writing. Three ways are detailed below, in the form of a handout for students. The first two are effective when a large body of literature needs to be reviewed since they provide ways of dividing up the task into more manageable chunks. Both benefit from fairly small, neat handwriting! The third is an exercise designed to help students to think about how their work is taking shape.

Organising information

Organising material for a project, dissertation or thesis can be a daunting task. Three ways to make this task manageable are described below.

1   Topic envelopes

This method is particularly useful if you are not clear at the outset how you want to organise your material. You will need some small file cards and a number of envelopes. When you read a published journal article or a chapter, summarise the important points on a file card, remembering to add the reference. When you have produced a number of summary cards, put those that relate to the same topic together in an envelope and write the topic on the outside of the envelope. When you come across further references on a particular topic put the summary cards into the appropriate envelope. When you begin writing, look at the cards in each envelope, organise the cards within an envelope and write about them in turn.

2   Review pad

This method is more appropriate if you have some idea of the main sections of your review and the likely order of the sections in the final version, but are uncertain about which references will go in each section. It is especially useful if you want to review a great deal of literature. You will need a pad of A4 paper.

First, decide on the sections and subsections of your review. Then, write the title of the first section/subsection at the top of the top sheet of paper. On the next sheet of paper write the title of the next section/subsection and so on, writing the sections in order. If you already know that there is a great deal of literature to be reviewed in one section, leave an additional blank page before the next section page. As you read the relevant literature make brief notes of each paper on the relevant section page, if necessary imposing some additional sectioning within the page if this becomes apparent, by, for example, writing a new section title half way down the page or on the back. Keep full details of each reference elsewhere. When you come to write the review, focus on one section at a time, read through the references noted on that page and, as they are reviewed, cross them off.

3   Pictures

If you are the kind of person who finds it easier to make sense of things when they are presented visually, you will probably find it helpful to organise your project material in the form of a diagram.

As you accumulate information for your project, look for ways of giving it a shape. Ask yourself if some bits connect with others or contrast with others, or are parallel to others, and how they all fit together to form the whole which is your topic.

Take a large sheet of paper and try to draw the topic in a way that shows these relationships. It may not make any sense to anyone else (see example opposite) but it should help you to see clearly how your information can be organised.

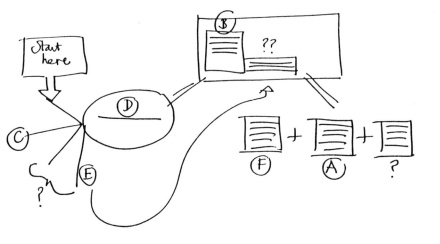

Improving undergraduate students' report writing   19

When students are required to write their first report of an experimental project they may find it very difficult, especially if they have had no experience of this sort of writing. Part of the difficulty arises because they do not know what is expected. One way to give them some idea of what is expected is to provide them with a report written by another student. However, although this may be useful to an extent, the report will be much more influential if you incorporate it into the following exercises. These exercises can be run successfully with a group of four or more students. (The first exercise could be modified for use with other types of writing.)

First, find a report which is not too long and moderately good (say a mid 2,2 standard). Get this typed up and copied so that each student can have a copy. Before you hand out the report explain the institution's marking system to the students.

How to run the exercises

Exercise 1: Marking a report

Individual work (15 minutes - vary according to the length of the report) Hand out the report and tell the students they have 15 minutes to
- read the report
- give it a mark using the institution's marking system
- identify two good points about the report
- identify two things which could be improved in the report.

In pairs (5 minutes)
Ask the students to compare their marks and to discuss the good and poor points and note any others which arise in the course of their discussion.

Plenary (10 minutes)
Ask the students for their marks and present these on an OHP. In the large group gauge from a show of hands how many gave it marks in each degree band.

Ask each pair in turn to identify one good point about the report. List these on an OHP. Go round the group until all the good points have been covered. Do the same for things that could be improved.

Tell the students what mark you would give the report (or the mark it obtained if that is known to you). Comment on the lists of good and poor aspects of the report and add any of yours which have not been mentioned. Point out any inconsistencies between marks given and points raised: for example, students have been known to give a report a first and, at the same time, identify a number of substantial problems with the write-up.

If there is time, continue with the following rewriting exercise.

Exercise 2: Rewriting a report

This exercise has been designed for a group of 16 students. For larger or smaller groups you will need to modify the stages.

Prior to the exercise identify and make photocopies of four reasonably short sections of the report which you feel would benefit from rewriting. Rewrite these sections yourself and produce a second handout containing these.

Individual work (10 minutes)
Each student spends 10 minutes rewriting one of the four sections (you can either negotiate which section each student rewrites or allocate them but ensure that a similar number of students tackle each section).

In pairs (10 minutes)
Each student pairs up with another student who has rewritten the same part of the report and they compare what they have written. Jointly they produce a further version of the section.

In fours (10 minutes)
Two pairs who have worked on the same section compare rewrites and modify them to produce an agreed version.

Plenary (15 minutes)
Ask a spokesperson from each group of four to read out their rewritten version. Hand out your version and discuss any major differences. Point out that there are lots of different ways of writing a good report.

Helping students to find a voice 20

The successful academic speaks and writes in a voice which, as well as being appropriate to his or her subject area, is also particular to the person and individually recognisable. This is true of academics in the sciences and social sciences as well as the arts and humanities.

Students embarking on an extended piece of writing such as a project report, dissertation or thesis need a consistent, strong and authentic voice in which to express themselves. You can help your students to find a voice by using one or more of the following methods.

- **The right questions**
  As a supervisor, keep asking your students 'What do *you* think?' or 'Where are *you* in all this?' Say 'How do *you* respond to *x*?' rather than 'What is *x*?' or 'What do you know about *x*?' Keep pressing them until you get a response that sounds authentic.

- **Notices**
  Suggest to your students that they stick a notice on their word processors saying 'What are *you* trying to say?'

- **Tape recordings**
  If your students make tape recordings of the discussions which they have with you and others about their academic work, they can analyse the tapes, not only with a view to developing the content of their topic but also in order to identify and define a voice. (In the early stages the voice may be colloquial and messy and therefore unacceptable as academic writing but it will have the tone and basic characteristics of the student's own voice.)

- **Models**
  Suggest to your students that in their reading they look out for a book or article which makes them think 'I'd like to write like that' or 'That

sounds like the kind of thing I could write' and use it as a model. You could even suggest that they practise writing in the style of that author by reading sections and then attempting to rewrite them from memory.

• **Comparisons**
Point out to your students how your own style differs from that of a colleague with whom they are also familiar.

Unblocking writer's block 21

When the time comes for students to start writing their dissertations or theses, it is not unusual for them to find themselves suffering from writer's block. This can take various forms: some students may protest that they are not yet ready to start writing; others may feel that their minds have gone blank; others again may just be in a state of panic.

Reasons for writer's block vary but students are certainly subjected to a lot of pressure at this stage. This may be the longest and weightiest piece of written work they have ever undertaken, it may count for more marks and represent more of a commitment than anything they have written before, and the long run-up period of preparatory reading, researching or experimenting can mean that the moment of putting pen to paper assumes a frightening importance.

As a supervisor you can be very helpful to students suffering from writer's block if you recognise it when it happens and employ one or more of the following methods to unblock it.

• **'Answer these questions'**
  In a case where the student's mind has gone blank, you can ask him some really fundamental questions about the dissertation, such as:
  Why did you choose this topic?
  What's the main thing you want to say?
  What other things do you want to say?
  If this dissertation/thesis works out the way you want it to, what might it be like?
  What are the main things you want a reader to take away from your dissertation/thesis?

  Questions such as these are easy for the student to answer and so help to rebuild his confidence.

- **'Write me a letter'**
  In a case where the student has plenty of ideas but sees formal academic language as a hurdle, he can be encouraged to write a letter to you (or to a friend or relative), telling you about the ideas but not worrying about how they are expressed. This can ease up the writing process for the student and once the ideas are on paper they can be rewritten in a more acceptable form.

- **'Write a rough draft'**
  In a case where the student imagines that the piece of writing must be perfect at the first attempt, you can suggest that he sees it instead as a rough draft, certainly to be rewritten and possibly to be scrapped altogether in the end. Your student may feel more encouraged to do this if you can show him a rough draft of your own, complete with insertions, crossings out and scribbles.

- **'Do it now'**
  In a case where the student is ready to write but is afraid of the first moment of commitment, you can say to him, 'Sit here at my desk. Take this pen and this paper and do it now' or 'Sit down at this computer and do it now'. A clear instruction of this kind can often make it possible for the student to get started.

- **'Talk into this tape recorder'**
  In a case where the student has plenty to say about the topic but is afraid of writing it down, you can ask him to make a tape recording of the material, either there and then in your office or later at home. Students who use this method are invariably surprised to find how much of the recorded material is subsequently usable.

- **'Start where you like'**
  In a case where the student feels blocked because he thinks that the only place to start writing is at the beginning but has not yet worked out how to begin, you can suggest that he postpones writing the

opening pages: since the function of an introduction is to introduce the whole piece, it is normally advisable to write it last. Suggest instead that he starts with an area from within the body of the thesis which interests him or which he feels relatively confident about.

If these methods work for your students, your best way of reinforcing their success is to praise their efforts and their courage.

If these methods do not work for your students, and they remain distressed, it is probably advisable to refer them to your department's study counsellor or your institution's counselling service.

Helping students to give oral presentations   22

Giving an oral presentation to a group of people can be a daunting experience, even for an established academic. It can be especially daunting the first time. Very often in higher education students, whether doing a first degree or a higher degree, have to give a talk about their work. They may be required or expected to give a talk to a small group of staff and students, to the entire department or school or, in the case of a student on a higher degree, to a conference meeting.

As a supervisor you can help your students prepare for such presentations.

If you are supervising a group of students, arrange a meeting at which all students give a brief account of their work. Suggest that each 'presentation' takes about five minutes with no interruptions and that individuals talk about their projects and any problems they are having.

If appropriate you might want to suggest beforehand that they consider using an OHP or handout to summarise the main points.

Afterwards be positive about the presentations. You are trying to make your students feel more at ease. Improvement will come with time.

If you have more than eight students, it is probably better to arrange two separate meetings; if you have only one student, suggest a joint meeting with a colleague and her students.

If students are required to give a presentation to a larger group of students and staff when the work is complete, try to arrange more than one meeting like the one described above. For example, if the work is completed over two terms, with a final presentation at the end of the second term, arrange one meeting about half way through the first term, a second meeting part way through the second term and a third meeting a couple of weeks before the required presentation. Suggest to your students that they use this third meeting as a rehearsal for the real thing.

If you are supervising research students, particularly doctoral students, and want to help them to give conference papers, there are several ways you can do this.

* Present papers at conferences yourself. Otherwise you cannot expect your students to do so.
* Encourage your students to attend conferences you are also going to. Discuss with them presentations you have both attended, including any of your own. What worked well? What did not work so well? Share any anxieties you have about giving papers.
* When they have completed sufficient research for a paper of their own suggest that they submit one to a conference. Devote a number of supervisions to planning the talk with your student. Two or three weeks before the conference suggest that he gives the paper to a small group of graduate students. Be positive and give him constructive feedback: point out what worked well and suggest ways in which he could improve specific aspects of the presentation. Be prepared to help him with the organisation of the talk, any visual aids etc. If necessary suggest that he gives a second informal presentation before the conference. You could also offer to video record the presentation so that he could watch it afterwards. If he takes you up on this offer let him have the video and allow him to watch it alone. Only watch it with him if he asks you to.

If possible arrange for him to give the paper to a group of other staff and students before the conference.

At the conference sit at the front with him. Be prepared to do part of the presentation if he would like you to. Be prepared to take his place if he feels unable at the last minute to do the presentation. Be prepared to help answer questions and to rescue him from difficult questions. Be as supportive as you can. Talk with him afterwards about how he felt giving the paper.

Writing jointly with research students   23

If you are supervising research students, it is likely that you will have published research papers and will have developed good writing skills. You can help the students you are supervising to improve their writing skills by suggesting that you write papers reporting their research findings jointly, with the student as the first author of any paper.

As well as enabling students to benefit from your experience of writing and publishing, writing jointly will have other advantages. Writing joint papers throughout the period of the degree will develop the students' writing skills, which will be of value when they come to write their theses. If you are committed to writing joint papers and encourage this in your students, it will increase the likelihood that they will have written up part of their work prior to writing their theses. Working jointly may lead to the development and furthering of ideas for additional questions or issues for the students to explore which might not have arisen during supervision.

Writing jointly may also increase your students' employability after they have completed their research degree. It will give them the experience of working collaboratively, evidence of which is increasingly sought in many professions. More specifically it may assist those research students, particularly those doing PhD, who want to pursue an academic career: the competition for academic posts is strong and increasingly appointment panels are looking for evidence of research publications.

Keeping students going

Reviewing progress 24

When a student embarks on a project, dissertation or thesis which has to be completed over one, two, three years or even longer, as may be the case for students doing a PhD part-time, he may feel that there is plenty of time. However it is easy for time to pass very quickly without the student progressing a great deal, or with the student spending a disproportionate amount of time on a small aspect of the topic, or with the student discovering that he has taken on a topic which is too big to be manageable. As the supervisor it is important that you monitor the available time and help your student plan his work efficiently. Several ways in which you can encourage students to plan are suggested below.

- **At the beginning**
  At the beginning of his period of study provide your student with some indication of the different phases. This could be in the form of a handout similar to the one which follows this item. This handout was produced for MSc students by the Higher Education Research Office at Auckland University in New Zealand and shows the various stages of the MSc period of study. It also gives some indication of how students may feel at particular points in time, which may enable them to talk more openly about their feelings later on (see item 28, *Supporting students emotionally*).

  In order to help your students to be realistic about how much they will be able to cover discuss with them topic areas, questions and titles which some of your previous students eventually settled on.

- **At the end of each meeting**
  At the end of each meeting allow five minutes to identify what the student will do by the next one. It may also be appropriate for you to agree something you will do yourself, in relation to the student's research. Make a note of these decisions. Spend the first few minutes when you next meet reviewing with the student whether or not he has

achieved his specified targets. If students set unrealistic targets which they fail to meet, guide them towards goals they can achieve.

• **Regularly**
  Encourage your students to monitor their own progress by suggesting they note down answers to the following questions:

  What have I completed so far?

  What aspects of the project or dissertation am I working on at the moment?

  What have I still got to do?

  What do I want to have done by next time?

  If the project or dissertation lasts at least a year it is appropriate to review progress in this way once every three months. Encourage your students to keep a record of their answers to compare with subsequent ones. In this way they can observe their own progress (or otherwise) and hopefully adjust their activities accordingly. You may also want to consider using a formal monitoring system based on similar principles (see item 35, *Records and reports*).

While the above methods can help students become more aware of their progress and what remains to be done, it is also important that as supervisor you provide an honest evaluation of what they have done and what remains to be done, within the context of the overall period of study (see also item 26, *Giving feedback to students*).

PROCESS MODEL FOR THE ONE-YEAR THESIS

1 - 3 months	*4 - 6 months*	*7 - 9 months*	*10 - 12 months*

• Selecting topic
• Reading around the area, theory and methodology
• Formulating a question
• Establishing supervision
	• Reading focussed around question
	• Drafting literature review
	• Reading for and planning method
	• Planning structure
	• Collecting Data
		• "Reading" Data
		• Drafting method and discussion sections
		• Reviewing structure
		• Collecting Data
			• Intensive writing phase:
			  - drafting & revising
			  - editing
			• Proofing and production

NOVEMBER - JANUARY	*FEBRUARY - APRIL*	*MAY - JULY*	*AUGUST - NOVEMBER*

T I M E   T H R O U G H

W R I T I N G

• Keeping a journal • Writing around a point, theory, etc	• Early drafting • Getting written feedback from supervisor • Getting oral feedback from supervisor and peers	• Intensive writing • Continuing feedback from supervisor and peers • Designing layout	

excitement · boredom · determination · insight · despair · relief

© Student Learning Centre, University of Auckland, 1993Ong

'How does this fit in?'   25

When students embark on projects, dissertations or theses they may be doing so for the first time and consequently have no personal experience of producing these sorts of reports. This is especially true of students carrying out research for a higher degree. Few, if any of us, produce more than one PhD. In contrast, as a supervisor, you will have some experience of such reports: you may have produced a report for a degree at the same level yourself and you may have supervised other students at the relevant level. This experience of seeing projects through to their completion is invaluable and can be put to good use in guiding your students towards writing a coherent final product.

One way of doing this is to keep reminding your students of the outcome of the project, namely the project write-up, dissertation or thesis. It is very easy for students to get so involved in the details of a study or literature review that they lose sight of how it relates to the end product. As a result they may waste valuable time on some aspect of the work which will contribute little or nothing to the final product. As a supervisor you need to keep a close check on whether what they are doing is contributing to the production of an acceptable piece of work within the given time. You can achieve this by asking the question 'How does this fit in?' when they suggest a new study, a different analysis or a review of a particular topic in the literature. If you do this each time your students suggest something new they will gradually take on board that the production of a coherent final report is critical if they are to complete successfully.

Giving feedback to students 26

Undergraduates are accustomed to receiving regular feedback, including numerical assessments, on their written coursework. They know how they are getting on in relation to their fellow students and in the context of the degree classification system. The situation may change, however, when they start working on an undergraduate project or dissertation or post-graduate thesis; it often happens that supervisors are content merely to correct drafts and offer vague encouragement, leaving the student short of really useful feedback.

The following well known principles of giving feedback apply as much to supervision as they do to any other learning situation.

- **The student should be invited to evaluate himself first.**
  Ask your student 'How do *you* think it's going?' The answer you receive will show you the student's view of the situation; you can use it as the basis for your own feedback. Encouraging the student to evaluate himself first fosters his self respect and encourages him to develop the skills of self criticism.

- **Feedback should be specific as well as general.**
  Students benefit from general feedback such as 'I'm really pleased with how this is taking shape' or 'This is going fine' or even 'I'm afraid this isn't good enough yet'. They also need specific feedback such as 'I specially like the way you've done x' or 'You could have improved this by developing y' or 'I suggest you reorganise this by examining a, b and c separately'. This mixture of feedback gives them something specific to focus on as well as offering them an overall picture of their progress.

- **Feedback should be written as well as spoken.**
  The advantage of written feedback is that the student can take it away and ponder it; the advantage of spoken feedback is that it has the

benefit of immediacy. Good feedback will consist of a mixture of the two.

- **Feedback should be balanced.**
  If your feedback to your students is totally positive, they may feel uncertain about how to improve their work; if it is wholly negative, they may feel demoralised. Balanced feedback can offer a way forward as well as praise and encouragement. A useful formula for balanced written feedback is:

  > Some things I like about your piece of work
  > Suggestions for improvement

- **Feedback should be given regularly and frequently.**
  Students need to know how they are getting on. Don't assume that your students can read your mind; tell them what you think of their work. And keep telling them.

Editing drafts 27

Editing students' drafts is a crucial part of the supervisor's role. A problem for students is that there is a lot of variation between supervisors as to how much editing they are prepared to do and of what kind and how quickly they return the work to the students.

Some supervisors do a thorough proofreading job, correcting all typographical, grammatical and stylistic errors while others leave those details to their students. Some supervisors make conceptual corrections, rewriting passages and substituting their own ideas, while others prefer to elicit ideas from their students by asking questions or recommending extra reading. Some supervisors are constantly pushing their students to do better while others are content to accept what their students have written.

Factors which should determine the extent and nature of your feedback are as follows.

• **The needs, commitment and capabilities of your students**
  Different students need and want different amounts and kinds of feedback on their drafts. Discuss their needs and wants with them so that you can be really clear about what you will be doing when you edit their drafts.

• **The concerns of your students**
  If you ask your students, each time they give you material to look at, to give you a note of their main concerns about what they have written and to specify what kind of feedback they would like, your editing can be better targeted and also less time-consuming for you.

• **The policy or conventions of your department**
  Your department may have a policy or, if not, will certainly have conventions about how much editing supervisors should do, and of what kind, and how quickly work should be returned to students.

Make sure that you adhere to any guidelines. If, for some reason, you cannot return work to students within the agreed time period, give them an explanation. Gross differences between supervisors are unfair on students and can be the basis for student appeals.

- **The recommendations of your external examiners**
  External examiners for undergraduate courses are in a good position to spot inconsistencies between colleagues and between institutions and often make very helpful recommendations.

- **The requirements of any external body**
  Some of these provide guidelines for supervisors.

- **The constraints on your time**
  If you find that you are spending too much time on editing drafts or giving feedback to particular students, you will need to analyse why this is happening and seek to negotiate a more realistic policy with your students or your colleagues.

(See also item 4, *Supporting postgraduate students from overseas.*)

Supporting students emotionally 28

Most supervisors are good at supporting students academically: they are academics themselves, and often experts on the topics they are supervising; they know how to manage their working environment and how to write scholarly prose. They may however be less good at supporting their students emotionally.

Here are some key questions to put to your students if you want them to feel supported as people and not just as supervisees.

- **'How's it going?'**
  This is a good question to ask at the beginning of a tutorial. Because it is so unspecific it gives the student freedom to take the conversation in the direction which is most helpful for him.

- **'How can I help?'**
  This is a question which you need to keep asking as supervisor. Don't assume that you know the best way to help: find out from your student what this is.

- **'Do you want to tell me about it?'**
  Many supervisors imagine that they need to be telling their student things all the time. In fact, tutorials will be more successful if the student is mostly talking and the supervisor is mostly listening.

- **'How do you feel?'**
  Unexpressed feelings get in the way of academic progress but students tend to assume that the expression of feelings is not allowed in an academic setting unless they are expressly invited to say how they feel. You can ask the student how he is feeling or, if you think a tentative interpretation of his feelings would be more supportive, you can say 'This seems to be worrying you' or 'You seem rather depressed'.

For many students the most supportive thing you can say is 'You can do it'. Over and over again.

The supervisor as mirror   29

As supervisor you need to find ways of helping your students to explore and clarify their ideas and feelings. A successful but unintrusive way of doing this is to act as a mirror and use the technique of reflection, borrowed from Rogerian counselling. This technique consists of reflecting back to the student his own ideas and feelings; the tutor can repeat the student's actual words or paraphrase them.

So, for example, if a student feels overwhelmed by the size of the task and says 'It all seems too much', you can acknowledge his feelings by reflecting the words 'Too much?' Said supportively, this enables the student to take the next step in exploring the difficulty.

Or, if a student loses sight of the overall direction or shape of the project, you can be very helpful in offering a summary of some of its main features. This needs to be expressed tentatively, prefaced with the words 'Would it be helpful if I summarised where I think you've got to?' and followed up with the question 'Is that a fair summary?'

Or, again, if a student is acting as if he has forgotten something he said earlier, you can remind him by asking 'You did say you wanted to look at *x*. Are you still interested in exploring it?'

Clearly you will find it easier to reflect your student's feelings and ideas if you keep careful notes of the outcomes of your tutorials.

Learning from experience   **30**

There is a tendency for students who are under pressure to try to deal with problems as they arise and once a crisis is over to move on to their next concern without reflecting at all on the experience. In this way psychological patterns, such as procrastination or panic, are repeated as long as the students do not find ways of dealing with them. This can happen particularly in the case of students who are working on individual projects, dissertations or theses because they are studying so much of their time in isolation.

Problems, crises and even failures do however provide opportunities for students to reflect productively and learn from their experience. You can be helpful to your students if you encourage in them this kind of awareness. You can give them feedback about their psychological patterns by saying 'I've noticed that this is what you often do' or 'You tend to react like this, don't you?' You can encourage them to begin to break away from the patterns if you ask ' How could you break this pattern?' or 'What have you learned from this painful experience?'

Research students' discussion group 31

Unlike undergraduates and postgraduates on taught courses who will be following a programme as part of a large group, postgraduates working towards a research degree may spend one, two, three or even more years studying a very narrow topic essentially on their own. As a result it is very easy for them to narrow their focus and feel isolated. One way in which you can help to minimise these problems is to encourage your students to meet together regularly. You can do this by setting up a monthly book/journal discussion group.

If you are supervising several students working on different topics in the same general area you could encourage them to form a group; if you are supervising only one student try to link up with other supervisors and their students. Arrange an initial brief meeting of interested staff and students and invite everyone to bring along suggestions of recently published books and journal articles which they would be interested in discussing. At the meeting draw up a list of books/articles which individuals would like to discuss and identify three or four to be discussed at subsequent meetings. You will also need to ask for volunteers to lead each discussion. It is obviously important to choose material that is of general interest to the group to increase the likelihood that members of the group other than the nominated discussant read the books/articles prior to the meeting. Agree some dates and times. After the meeting circulate a list of the arranged meetings, indicating the book/article and lead discussant for each.

As well as putting students in contact with one another on a regular basis such a group will encourage your students to keep up to date with developments in areas which are broader than their specific thesis topic. Such opportunities can be very important in enabling students to relate their specific area of interest to the wider discipline area; this may be particularly valuable to them when they are writing up their thesis.

(See also item 47, *The isolated postgraduate student*.)

What next? 32

Students, whether taking an undergraduate or postgraduate course, are often uncertain about what to do when they finish and this may concern and preoccupy them. In addition many students underestimate their own abilities and, as a consequence, may restrict their options. If you are supervising their projects, dissertations or theses and have worked closely with them, you are likely to have a clear impression of their strengths and limitations. You may therefore be in a good position to discuss their choices with them, particularly the option of continuing in higher education, either by taking further courses or seeking employment within it. Students will perceive your interest and encouragement very positively.

You should be able to advise undergraduates on appropriate ways of pursuing their research or dissertation topic at a more advanced level. You should be able to inform them about appropriate postgraduate courses, and procedures for applying for courses and funding. In the case of students considering applying for a research degree you can help them identify the research area they are interested in and find potential supervisors in your own and other departments.

If you are supervising postgraduates, particularly at research degree level, it is helpful to discuss their future plans with them early on in their final year. If they would like to continue in research you can help them in several ways:

- You can put them in touch with other academics working in the same area. (If you have encouraged your students to attend conferences and present papers and posters they may have already made some useful contacts.)

- You can bring to their attention any research or lecturing opportunities that are advertised or which you hear about from colleagues.

- You can discuss the possibility of extending their research by applying for funding to cover their salary and any associated costs of the research. (Applying for funding usually involves quite a lengthy process, normally at least six months, which is one reason why you should discuss future plans with students well in advance of their completion dates.)

Looking after yourself

Managing time constraints 33

Many academics these days identify shortage of time as their main professional problem. As student numbers have increased, so the time available for individual students has diminished. This can lead to frustration and stress on the part of both supervisors and students unless measures are taken to counteract its effect.

- **Time in groups**
  There are certain basics which all students need to know before they can make any progress with their work. The details of these depend on the subject area and level of study but they include information on regulations and requirements, and advice on the skills of researching and writing (see items 14 and 15). If you tell students about these things in groups, not only will you save yourself time and needless repetition but also the students will benefit from the opportunity to question and discuss them together, both during the session and subsequently. (See also item 38, *Supervising students in groups*.)

- **Time with other people**
  If the time that your students have with you is insufficient for them, encourage them to talk about their work to anyone else who is willing to listen. Flat mates are good for this. Even if they know nothing about the topic they will often be able to offer general support and listen patiently while the student talks things through.

- **Quality time**
  Encourage your students to make the best use possible of the limited time they have with you. They can do this by preparing thoroughly for their tutorials: at the end of each tutorial you can both decide what the student should do for the next tutorial. (Be sure to make a note of this so that you remember what you are supposed to be covering and can prepare appropriately beforehand.) You can support students during the tutorials by giving them your full attention and in particular by

putting a *Do not disturb* notice on your door and by switching off the bell on your telephone or transferring your calls.

- **Tape recorded materials**
  If you have a substantial amount of information or feedback to give to a student you may be able to save time by tape recording it.

- **Making a complaint**
  If the time allowed for supervision is inadequate, you can get together with other colleagues and make a complaint; this will carry a lot of weight if it is backed up by educational and practical arguments. If you are overworked to the extent that your hours exceed those on your contract, your union officer will be pleased to help you fight this.

Using colleagues 34

Because of the nature of supervision, supervisors and students can easily find themselves locked into an exclusive relationship, cut off from outside support. It is easy for both supervisors and students to assume that supervisors must single-handedly cater for all the needs of the students.

There are however important ways in which your colleagues can support you in the supervisory role.

- **Referring students to colleagues**
  If aspects of your students' work are outside your range of expertise, as can happen with tutors who have large numbers of dissertations to supervise, you can refer students to colleagues with the necessary background and interests. As supervisor it is your job to oversee the *process*; it is quite appropriate for aspects of the *content* to be provided by colleagues.

- **Talking things through with colleagues**
  If you have doubts about your students' work, it can help to talk things through with a colleague and get some feedback.

- **Peer appraisal**
  The process of talking things through, if slightly formalised, can be developed into peer appraisal: you and a colleague of your choice can observe, or listen to a tape recording of, some of each other's supervision tutorials. (You will of course need the permission of the students involved.)

Records and reports 35

It is all too easy to adopt a fairly relaxed approach to supervising a student, especially if the student is registered for a higher degree. If you meet with the student regularly and each time there appears to be adequate progress it probably feels unnecessary to keep any records. Nevertheless, however well things seem to be going it is important to keep a record of each meeting which includes the date, a summary of the main points discussed and a note of any decisions made and targets agreed. In most cases these will just be 'for the record' but they may be invaluable should a query be made concerning your supervision by the student, your department, your institution or an external funding agency.

As well as keeping a record of each meeting it is useful to develop a system of interim reports. Monitoring of this kind provides useful feedback for the tutor and the students and also for the person who has the job of co-ordinating dissertations or theses.

These reports may be of two main types:

a the supervisor writes reports on the students' progress
b the students write reports on their own progress

You can set up type (a) or type (b) or a combination of the two types. The Psychology Department at Warwick University requires research students to provide details of what they have achieved and what they plan to do next on a form once every two months. The form is printed at the end of this item. Such a form has the advantage that both the supervisor and the student sign it to indicate that they agree with the dates of their meetings, the student's progress in the last two months and the student's plans for the next two months. Alternatively you might produce a proforma like the second one which follows this item and which has spaces for reports written by the tutor and the student on the same sheet.

As well as keeping records of progress it is also important that you note any concerns as soon as you become aware of them. Interim reports can be very helpful in highlighting any difficulties which students are encountering and in identifying whether there is a continuing problem. In general, if you feel unable to resolve a problem which is affecting a student's progress it is important to put something in writing as well as discussing the situation with the student. Your written report might take the form of a letter to the student expressing your concern or a confidential note to your head of department or school or other appropriate person. Many institutions will have committees to whom such concerns can be addressed (see item 36, *Postgraduate Supervisory Committee*).

If undergraduate students have to carry out a final year research project or dissertation on a topic of their own choosing, it is useful to require that they give an interim verbal report of their work to other students and perhaps a small group of staff, about two months before the submission deadline. Such presentations are of value for three main reasons. First, if students know that they are going to have to make a presentation when they start on the project, they are less likely to leave the research until the last minute, using the presentation date as an interim deadline. Second, the presentations should allow the students to obtain some feedback on their work from both staff and students which can be incorporated into the final write-up. Third, such presentations provide an opportunity for helping students develop their skills at communicating orally (see item 22, *Helping students to give oral presentations*). Given that students often put a lot of time and effort into making these sorts of presentations you might want to consider apportioning some of the final marks to the presentation, perhaps 10 to 20%.

UNIVERSITY OF WARWICK
Department of Psychology
BIMONTHLY PROGRESS REPORT BY RESEARCH STUDENTS

Deadline for receipt of this report by supervisor:	Date:	Last bimonthly report received:

SUPERVISOR(S)

DATES OF MEETINGS WITH SUPERVISORS

Brief summary of your activity and progress since your last bimonthly report. Please note any problems that have occurred and absence due to illness.

What goals have you set yourself for the next two-month period?

Student's signature:	Supervisor's signature:
Dated:	Dated:

PLEASE RETURN THIS FORM TO YOUR SUPERVISOR WHO WILL RETURN IT TO THE PSYCHOLOGY OFFICE

INTERIM REPORT

Award	Year
Name of student	Name of supervisor

Student's interim report

signed   *date:*

Supervisor's interim report

signed: *date:*

Postgraduate Supervisory Committee   **36**

At the undergraduate level, students' work is marked by a number of different staff over the course of each year and there is usually a yearly meeting of an exam board consisting of both internal and external examiners who oversee the procedures and results. The situation is often very different for postgraduate students, especially those registered for a research degree lasting more than one year. They may have only one supervisor and no-one other than that supervisor may read anything that they write until their thesis is submitted and sent to internal and external examiners. Such an arrangement is not ideal, either for the student or the supervisor. One way to improve the situation for both staff and students is to set up a postgraduate supervisory committee specifically to monitor progress. Such a committee was set up in the Department of Psychology at Warwick University some years ago and the way in which it operates is described below.

All research students in psychology at Warwick have their own postgraduate supervisory committee. In each case the committee consists of three members of academic staff, excluding the student's own supervisor(s), and including at least one and preferably two experienced supervisors, one of whom is appointed as chair. In June each year the Director of Postgraduate Studies (see item 3, *Recruiting research students*) writes to all research students and asks them to submit a brief report on their work over the previous year, identifying any problems which have affected their progress. In addition students may submit drafts of papers or chapters as well as a list of conferences attended, papers presented etc. Students are also asked to outline their plans for the following year and, if they are in their penultimate year, to submit a draft outline of their thesis chapters. The Director of Postgraduate Studies also writes to the supervisor(s) asking for a report, including any recommendations for upgrade, for example from MPhil to PhD (see item 5, *Which research degree?*) All reports have to be submitted by the end of June.

During July meetings are arranged between all students and their post-graduate supervisory committees. At each meeting, which usually last about 30 minutes, the committee discusses progress with the student and explores any concerns which have been mentioned either by the student or supervisor(s). After the meeting the chair writes a report on behalf of the committee, including such issues as whether or not it supports an upgrade. If the committee is concerned about some aspect of a student's progress or the nature of the supervision being provided, the report will recommend a course of action. This might be for an additional supervisor to be appointed or for the student to meet the committee to review progress in six months' time (rather than 12 months' time). The report is then given to the Director of Postgraduate Studies who passes it to the supervisor(s) and head of department. The Director of Postgraduate Studies is responsible for ensuring that any recommendations made by the committees are carried out.

This committee structure for monitoring progress, along with bimonthly reports on progress and plans (see item 35, *Records and reports*), has been associated with almost all postgraduate research students registered in psychology at Warwick submitting on time. It seems very likely that these monitoring systems have contributed to the high submission rate.

Different practices

Joint supervising 37

Joint supervision can be very beneficial to a student. The supervisors can also gain a great deal. However joint supervision is not without its difficulties and should not be entered into without a great deal of thought. Before embarking on such an arrangement explore how you and your intended co-supervisor feel about joint supervision using the following questions as a guide. If you cannot discuss the questions easily, then you should seriously consider abandoning the idea of supervising together!

•   **Do you trust and respect the other supervisor?**
    Although your aim may be for all supervisions to be joint there will be times when only one of you can meet the student. On such occasions it is important that the other supervisor has confidence in how the supervision will be handled and the advice which might be offered to the student.

•   **Can you communicate regularly?**
    Students will not always be able, or willing, to talk to both supervisors and so it is crucial that co-supervisors can keep each other up to date with the student's progress.

•   **Can you share your concerns?**
    When difficulties arise in the supervision of a student it is best if these are dealt with as soon as possible so that they do not develop into something more serious. If you have a concern about a student, it is essential that you can express this to your co-supervisor and that you can agree how to deal with the difficulty.

•   **Can you share the responsibilities?**
    It is easy with joint supervision for things to be left undone because each supervisor assumes that the other one is dealing with a problem or question. It is often helpful if you can agree at the outset how you are going to share the responsibilities of the supervision. For example,

in a practical project, one of you might make a major contribution to the statistical analyses, the other to the arrangements for locating participants. As questions arise during the course of the project it is important that you agree who will take responsibility for particular issues.

• **Can you be honest with your co-supervisor?**
Tensions will arise which will not benefit the student if you are not able to state openly when you disagree with something your co-supervisor (or the student) proposes. Because of this difficulties can emerge if the two supervisors are of very different status.

• **Can you regularly meet together with the student?**
If one of you has so many other commitments that the other will carry out most of the supervisions on her own, resentment may develop.

• **Do you share similar objectives for supervision?**
In order not to give students misleading messages joint supervisors should agree on the objectives of the supervision. Difficulties will arise if, for example, one of you thinks that supervisions are solely for tossing around ideas, while the other thinks that supervisions are for reviewing progress and agreeing on how to proceed.

• **Do you have specific skills to offer the supervision?**
Although it might be enjoyable to share the supervision of a student this alone cannot justify the additional time involved. If you and your co-supervisor have very similar skills, joint supervision may be unnecessary. If you have different but complementary skills, joint supervision may be very effective.

• **Do you have similar views?**
If you and your co-supervisor have a similar, though not identical, view of the topic, joint supervision may work well. On the other hand if your views are diametrically opposed, joint supervision may be disastrous for you and, more importantly, for the student.

Supervising students in groups   38

Students at any level can benefit from learning in a group, trying out their ideas on their peers and giving one another feedback and support. Whether you are obliged to supervise your students in groups because of increasing numbers and declining resources or whether you choose this method for its potential benefits to learning, there are methods of organising the sessions which are different from those which are suitable for one-to-one tutorials or group discussions.

- **Question and answer sessions**

  Students producing independent pieces of work can easily feel uncertain and insecure. They need to be able to reassure themselves by asking questions and receiving full answers. You can meet this need by organising regular question and answer sessions for groups of students, or perhaps by asking 'Any questions?' at the beginning of each group session. Students working as a group will benefit because some will ask questions which others would not have thought of asking or not dared to ask.

- **Progress reports**

  It is helpful to set aside some time periodically for students to reflect on how they are getting on, what they have achieved and what their next step is to be. They could do this in a round or in pairs. A useful format might be

  > What I have achieved so far/since the last progress report
  > What I intend to do next
  > How I feel about it

- **Problem solving sessions**

  When students meet problems they can benefit from having a group on hand to help them tackle them. This can be the whole group or, if it is too large, a subgroup. A problem-solving session characteristically consists of a statement of the problem by the individual student, followed by questions from the group which encourage the individual to clarify and refine the problem and concluding with solutions or suggestions from the rest of the group and from the individual himself. It is a good idea to have problem solving sessions as part of your regular group meetings.

- **'Workshopping'**
This method is most often used in the teaching of creative writing but is suitable for any situation where students in a group produce written work. The method consists of students in turn presenting a piece of writing to the group and receiving feedback. You can vary the format in a number of ways: the individual student can present his work either by reading it out or by distributing photocopies of it; the other students can present their feedback either in written form or orally; the group can work either as one group or in subgroups. In any case it is crucial that the students agree their guidelines for giving feedback: they could use the list in item 26, *Giving feedback to students*, as a starting point.

- **Working in pairs**
Students in a group benefit from having interludes when they can claim the undivided attention of another person in order to talk through something of particular importance to them. This is especially the case when their supervision is entirely in a group and they have no one-to-one sessions with the tutor. You can organise work in pairs on a regular basis. Just say, 'Now you've got five minutes each in pairs to talk something through'. If there is an odd number of students, pair up with someone yourself. Remember to time the two sessions and tell the students when they should change roles between speaker and listener and when they should finish.

Undergraduate students doing joint projects   39

In many subject areas undergraduate student numbers have increased markedly without corresponding increases in staff numbers. One of the consequences of this reduction in the staff:student ratio is that students carrying out individual projects and dissertations, with each student requiring individual supervision, can become too costly in terms of staff time. If, as a department, you wish to retain these important learning opportunities you will need to think of different ways of organising them. One solution is to require students to carry out their research projects or dissertations in pairs or threes. This will have the advantage that supervision of two or even three students will take about as much time as supervision of one student in the past, thus saving staff time. A further advantage of such an arrangement is that students will have the opportunity to develop their skills of working as part of a team, evidence of which is often sought by prospective employers. They will also benefit from the sorts of discussion and development of ideas which occur in teams.

However if you decide to require students to work on projects or dissertations in pairs or threes, you need to have clear guidelines about which parts of the work they can do jointly. It is obviously important to stress to the students that although they are carrying out the research jointly and may assign different tasks to different members of the group, their final write-ups must be independent.

It is also important to stress the need for all the students to contribute to the project. One way to encourage this is to ask each student to indicate how much each member of their group has contributed to the different phases of the research. This can be done by getting each student to complete a questionnaire similar to the one printed at the end of this item and hand it in with their final write-up. You can take this a step further by allocating a proportion of the marks for the project or dissertation to each group and asking them to divide the marks among themselves to reflect any differences in contribution. Thus you might assign 3% per student, so that if two students work together they have 6% to divide between them, three students have 9% and so on. When you have marked the final reports you then add on each student's allocation to get a final mark for each student.

3rd Year Project
Student's assessment of partner's help

Project title:
Student id: Supervisor:

Was the project carried out with a partner?   Yes/No

If the project was carried out with a partner, you must submit the following form, completed, with your project report. You should not collaborate with your partner in completing the form. Each partner must submit their own form with their report.

Did both of you contribute to all phases of the project? Yes/No

Now please use the following scales to assess the relative contribution made by you and your partner.

		Mainly by me				Mainly by partner
1	Originality of topic	1	2	3	4	5
2	Theoretical contribution	1	2	3	4	5
3	Research design	1	2	3	4	5
4	Procedure and technique	1	2	3	4	5
5	Data analysis & stats	1	2	3	4	5
6	Interpretation of results	1	2	3	4	5
7	Literature referenced	1	2	3	4	5
8	Workload involved in project	1	2	3	4	5

Signature: _____

Additional comments: (continue overleaf if necessary)

Reciprocity 40

Disparity of power is an important issue in supervision. The power lies with the supervisor who, as tutor, advisor and often examiner, can easily make the mistake of organising the supervisory relationship in a way which allows the student very little autonomy. The student, meanwhile, will often assume the complementary deferential role. This can lead to the production of a project, dissertation or thesis whose shape and emphasis are more the tutor's than the student's own and in which the student's ideas, interests and creativity are suppressed.

As supervisor, look for ways of reducing the disparity of power between you and your student. One way of doing this is to introduce reciprocity into the relationship. Some suggestions for ways of doing this follow. (The first two suggestions focus on the student's work; the other two are broader based and will only be successful if the student is the kind of person who is open to experimenting with practices of this kind. They will also generally work better if the time you allow for the student is longer than the time you take for yourself.)

- **Reciprocal reading lists**
  Instead of simply providing your student with a reading list, you can propose exchanging lists. You could say, 'I'll suggest some books and articles for you to read and I'd like you to give me a list of references which I need to read if I'm to understand how you see this project and what your particular interests are'.

- **Reciprocal reports**
  It is a good idea for you and your student to report on each other periodically: you can give him feedback on his research findings and written drafts and he can evaluate you as supervisor. This may happen formally or informally and orally or in writing. If you set this up occasionally as a reciprocal exercise, you will both be under less pressure and feel less exposed. You could say, 'I'd like to give you

some feedback about how I think your work is progressing and I'd like some feedback from you about how I'm doing as a supervisor. What I suggest is that next time we meet we take a few minutes each to do this. I'm telling you now so that we've got time to think beforehand about what we want to say'.

- **Reciprocal supervision**
  Another way of reducing the disparity of power is to reverse roles with your student for part of the tutorial: first you listen to him talking about his work and then he listens to you talking about something for which you need a willing listener, such as a journal article you are writing or a new course you are teaching. It could even sometimes happen that you both want to explore the same topic, such as time management. Or if the two of you were writing a paper jointly you might find it helpful to read out your contributions to each other. Additional advantages of this practice are that you are modelling for your student the way an experienced academic thinks; you and your student will each gain an insight into the role of the other, which will help you to play your primary roles with more understanding; and the student will also gain particular experience of the supervisory role, which may be an asset to him in his future career.

- **Reciprocal reading**
  As well as reading your students' drafts, ask them to read things that you write, such as conference papers or grant applications. They will appreciate being treated as colleagues and you both stand to gain from the experience.

Supervising postgraduate students at a distance 41

Situations will arise where it is not possible for you to meet face to face all the time with your students: you may move institutions and still continue as an external supervisor; your students may be part-time and spend much of their time working elsewhere; as part of their studies your students may need to work in another institution, in another part of the country or in a different country; you may be away for a period of time or too busy to see your students. When these and similar situations arise it is necessary to develop ways of supervising other than the traditional face to face meeting. Some of these alternatives are described below. Some are similar to face to face supervising in that the communication is occurring in real time; the others are different in that they do not rely on all parties being available at a given time.

- **Post**

  It is important that all students, especially those undertaking a research degree, produce written material. This may range from a rough outline of the questions or issues to be addressed in the thesis to a draft of a chapter or proposed interpretations of some data collected. A written response from the supervisor is very valuable when working at a distance. A great deal of progress can be made if students regularly send written material and supervisors respond with written comments. Obviously for this arrangement to be most effective it is important that supervisors are able to provide feedback very rapidly.

- **Telephone/telephone conferencing**

  In the past the telephone has been the most usual way of maintaining contact over a distance. It can be useful for obtaining quick answers to straightforward questions. It is also possible to connect three or more people by telephone which might be useful if you are engaged in joint supervision of a student at a distance. However as soon as more than two people are connected by telephone it is important to establish certain ground rules for the conversation: establish an agenda at the outset so that you can all be clear what needs to be covered; do not interrupt before the person speaking has finished making a point; make points succinctly; check to see if others want to say something. It is also useful if one of you agrees to circulate a note of the main points after the call has ended.

In some areas it is already possible for telephone conferencing to be linked to video so that the different participants can see one another as well as hear one another. Such arrangements make the communication more like a face to face situation although it is still useful to agree some basic ground rules.

- **Electronic mail/conferencing**
  Most, if not all, higher education institutions provide staff and students with access to computers and electronic mail (email). Electronic mail enables messages to be sent from one computer to another within seconds anywhere in the world provided that both computers have the necessary connections. This method has a number of advantages over the telephone, particularly if long distances over different time zones are involved, since email does not require that your correspondent is sitting at his or her computer at the time you send your message: sent messages are stored and picked up by the addressees when they next check their mail on their computers. Provided that both you and your students have email addresses this can be a very efficient way to communicate. You can also set up groups of addresses so that the same message can be sent to everyone in the group.

If you have a number of students it may be useful to indicate to them that there will be a particular time of day or a particular day of the week when you will check your email messages and reply to them.

It is now possible to set up electronic versions of telephone conferencing. This enables a group of people to communicate with one another electronically. The group decides when to meet (electronically speaking) and a supervision can be held with each person contributing and commenting in turn. You should check what systems are available in your institution with the person responsible for information technology.

Assessment

Role play viva 42

If your students are to be examined by vivas, it is important that you offer them practice in being assessed in this way, particularly since for many of them this will be their first experience of an examination of this type.

You and your colleagues can set up practice sessions yourselves with individual students or organise pairs of students to role play with each other. A description of both types of session follows. Whichever type you choose, you will need to begin the session by inviting students to talk about vivas and ask questions about them. The best way you can respond is by answering their questions fully and reassuring them about their anxieties.

Option 1: Supervisor & student

a   *Either* prepare a list of viva questions to ask the student
    or ask the student to prepare a set of viva questions for you to put.

b   Rearrange the furniture in your office so that it looks more formal or use a different room, more like the one where the viva will be held.

c   Do the role play thoroughly, including asking the student to wait outside and knock on the door before coming in.

d   During the role play, ask the questions and listen to the answers but don't give feedback to the student. Make notes if you need to.

e   Signal the end of the role play by saying, 'That's the end of the role play. Now let's move on to the feedback'.

f   Ask the student to evaluate the viva first and build your feedback onto his. You can encourage him to start by asking 'How do you think you did?'

Option 2: Pairs of students
(This can be done with any number of pairs working simultaneously.)

a   If the students are familiar with one another's work, ask them to formulate a list of interesting questions to put to their partners. If not, ask them to write a set of challenging questions on their own work for their partners to put to them.

b   Explain to them the importance of being clear when they are in role and out of role.

c   Tell them how much time you are allocating for the role play (say 10 minutes the first time they do the exercise, increasing later to the actual time of the viva). Announce when the role play is starting and stopping.

d   At the end of the role play ask the student playing the candidate to evaluate his own performance and then ask the other member of the pair to offer feedback.

e   Ask the pairs to swap the roles of examiner and candidate and run the exercise again.

If you have the facilities you could make audio or video recordings of the role plays to offer your students another, different type of feedback.

Second marking procedure for undergraduate 43
projects and dissertations

Despite increasing pressures on staff, undergraduate projects and dissertations are often marked by two examiners, one of whom is normally the
supervisor and the other a second member of staff. Supervisors will know
more about the projects or dissertations than the second markers. For
example, they will know whether the ideas for the work were entirely the
students'; whether they read and commented on drafts; whether they
helped the students in other ways. The supervisors will also be better able
to judge whether the studies involved more or less work than average. It
is important that your department decides whether this information should
contribute to the marks awarded. If the final product is being marked and
no account is to be taken of any help which may have been given, then it
is essential that the second marker is unaware of it. (The advantage of this
way of marking is that students are not discouraged from seeking help if
they need it.) However if the marks are to take account of how much help
the students have had then it is important that the information available to
the supervisors is passed to the second markers.

The simplest and fairest way to do this is for supervisors to fill in a form
for each project or dissertation indicating how much help was given. A
form which has been used to do this for undergraduate projects is
reproduced at the end of this item.

Your department also needs to decide the impact that various kinds and
amounts of help should have on the marks. For example, you might decide
that projects and dissertations should be marked as they stand and that a
certain percentage should be deducted subsequently for specific help. One
possibility would be to deduct 5% from each mark if the idea for the project
or dissertation was suggested by the supervisor. An alternative would be
to give additional marks if the idea originated from the student. Indeed it
would be possible to devise a system where each area in which help could
be given was allocated a certain percentage of the marks.

2nd Year Project
Supervisor's assessment of help provided
Project title:
Student id: Supervisor:
                               Second marker:

How many partners did this student have?   **2   1   0**

If the student had any partners, is an evaluation of their contribution completed
by this student attached?   **Yes   No**
If not, please contact the student urgently and ask them to complete a form. Note
the date the form was eventually received.

What is your evaluation of the relative contribution of this student compared
to their partner(s), if they had any?

            100 ——————— 50 ——————— 0
This one...   Did it all   Did nothing

Now use the following scales to assess the relative contribution made by this
student and the project supervisor.

	Suggested to Student		Normal help		Entirely S's own
1 Originality of topic	1	2	3	4	5
2 Theoretical contribution	1	2	3	4	5
3 Research design	1	2	3	4	5
4 Procedure & technique	1	2	3	4	5
5 Data analysis & stats	1	2	3	4	5
6 Interpretation of results	1	2	3	4	5
7 Literature referenced	1	2	3	4	5
8 Workload involved in project	Light		Normal		Heavy
	1	2	3	4	5

Additional comments by supervisor (overleaf)
Remarks on the student's performance, discrepancies between 1st & 2nd marks, comments on
student's own evaluation of their relative contribution, etc.

Choosing examiners for research degrees 44

If you supervise postgraduate students registered for research degrees, you will normally be asked to recommend internal and external examiners. This request will usually come from the central administration in your institution and will be prompted by the student indicating his intention to submit. However it is useful to consider possible examiners before this point.

The selection of internal and external examiners is an important part of the supervision process and should be taken seriously. It is worth identifying and discussing potential external examiners with each student fairly early on. Although a thesis should not be written for a particular examiner (since a preferred examiner may not be available when the thesis is finally submitted and an alternative will have to be found) it can be helpful for students to have in mind likely examiners when they are writing up. You should also ask your students if they have any suggestions, though it is you (or the head of your department) who makes the recommendation, not the student.

In identifying appropriate examiners it is important to consider the relative expertise of the internal and external examiners and aim for a balance between the two. Ideally they should both have experience of supervising postgraduates at the level of the proposed thesis. In fact most institutions have guidelines for the appointment of examiners: you will need to check these. There may be very little choice for the internal examiner but there will be a wide choice for the external. One examiner (preferably the external) should have expertise which is directly relevant to the research covered in the thesis. Your aim in choosing the internal (if there is any choice) should be to complement this expertise. You also need to select an internal who will make sure that the examination is fair and that appropriate procedures are followed. At least one of the examiners should be sympathetic to any specific difficulties associated with the student's research.

You also need to select examiners who are respected: the examination of a research thesis is a responsible job and you need to do your best to ensure that you choose people who will carry out the task conscientiously and thoroughly. If the examination involves a viva it is important that the examiners are able to discuss the student's work with authority.

You should not recommend anyone as an examiner, either internal or external, who has been closely connected with either the work reported in the thesis or the student. This is in order to minimise the likelihood of bias occurring (either for or against the student).

Examining research theses 45

If you are supervising postgraduate research students, sooner or later you will be asked to examine a research thesis either written by a student in your own university (as an internal examiner) or by a student in another university (as an external examiner). Different universities have different requirements about the experience which an examiner, internal or external, must have before taking on this sort of examining but normally you need to have successfully supervised at least one student to the level at which you are examining.

If you are invited to examine a research thesis it is important that you make a decision quickly as to whether or not you can take on the work. The amount of work that is necessary will obviously depend on the degree level being examined and the quality of the thesis but will seldom take less than a day and may well take several days.

The nature of your role will vary depending on whether you are the internal or external examiner. The university should provide you with guidelines of what is expected and you need to familiarise yourself with these. For example, if you are the internal examiner it is normal practice that you liaise with the external examiner and organise the viva if necessary. Very often both examiners have to provide independent reports on the thesis as well as a joint report. Your particular subject area may also be provided with guidelines on how to examine research theses and you should familiarise yourself with these too.

At an early stage you also need to be clear about the range of decisions available to you. This range is normally:

either a) the degree is awarded;

or b) the degree is awarded subject to minor amendments specified by the examiners and to be checked by the internal examiner;

or   c) the degree is not awarded but the student is allowed to resubmit the thesis amended along the lines suggested by the examiners within a specified time limit. In this case a second viva may be required if one was held initially;

or   d) the degree for which the thesis was submitted is not awarded but a degree of a lower level is awarded (MPhil in place of PhD; MSc/MA in place of MPhil);

or   e) the degree is not awarded.

When you have agreed to examine a thesis you will need to put aside an appropriate amount of time in which to read it and write your report, bearing in mind the possible final decision.

If there is to be a viva, it is important that you prepare thoroughly for it and do this sufficiently in advance of the date set that if you require any further information from either the student or the supervisor you have time to request it: try to read the thesis for the first time about two weeks before the date of the viva; put aside a whole day for this and try to ensure that you are not interrupted. As you read the thesis keep notes towards your report as well as a list of corrections which the student may be required to make. You probably do not need to read a thesis more than once. Having read the thesis and built up a set of notes use these to identify a number of general points of concern which can form the basis of the viva if there is to be one and can eventually be incorporated into your examiner's report.

After you have read the thesis, drafted your report and reached a provisional decision you will need to discuss your view of the thesis with the other examiner. If a viva is not required you will then need to write a joint report. If a viva is required you will need to discuss it with the other examiner. The external examiner usually takes the lead in the viva, although both examiners will contribute and both should have prepared thoroughly, identifying key questions to be asked.

The format followed in vivas varies between institutions: sometimes the supervisors are present, sometimes they are not; sometimes the examiners meet with the supervisors before the viva, sometimes after the viva, sometimes not at all.

Think carefully about how you arrange the room: try to avoid the situation where both examiners sit on one side of the table with the candidate on the other side. Think about how you will begin the viva: it is often useful to make some general statement and then to invite the student to build on it. Given that the viva is part of the examination process examiners cannot tell the candidate at the outset what the likely outcome is. However it is important to try to put the student as much at ease as possible and, provided that you are fairly sure that the degree will be awarded (even if some amendments may have to be made), try to say something which indicates that you feel the thesis is of the expected standard and that the student has examined some interesting issues in a competent way. It is also useful to outline to the student the format that the viva is likely to take.

Throughout the viva remember that you and the other examiner are going to have to write a joint report afterwards. It is important that you are agreed about any parts of the thesis that need to be amended so that you can make a clear recommendation to the board of examiners and thence to the student.

Normally a viva will last between one and two hours. Sometimes it is useful to have a break part way through so that you and the other examiner can discuss how it is going, identify issues which still need to be discussed and address any problems which have arisen.

When the viva has finished you will need to spend time discussing it with the other examiner. After you have reached a decision you may want to convey this informally to the candidate though you need to make clear that it is provisional and subject to the ratification of the appropriate body in the institution. It is absolutely crucial that you do not say anything that might mislead the candidate.

You will then need to draft and agree your final report with the other examiner and submit it to the university, along with your expenses claim form.

Giving marks for each stage of undergraduate projects and dissertations   **46**

The final version of the project report or dissertation is generally seen as a complete, discrete piece of work which therefore carries 100% of the marks allocated. This puts all the emphasis on the final product and a lot of strain on students, especially those who tend to leave everything until the last minute.

An alternative way of assessing the work is for your department to agree to allocate a proportion of the marks (say, 10 - 20% of the total) to interim progress reports, drafts or oral presentations. This entails extra work for staff but does encourage students to take these other aspects seriously and develop different skills. If deadlines are given for each stage, this helps students to pace themselves. It also gives them extra feedback on their progress.

When things go wrong

The isolated research student   47

It is very easy for students in higher education to feel isolated: they may have relatively little class contact with fellow students doing the same course and they may find it difficult to discuss their work with others. Such difficulties may be accentuated in project and dissertation work since these often require students to identify their own topic to research which means that they may be working on a problem quite different from those of their fellow students. Isolation of this sort may be even more marked in students carrying out research for a higher degree, particularly at the levels of MPhil and PhD. Here no-one else in the department may be working on the same problem. In addition there may be relatively small numbers of students in each year of study for a higher degree. It can be hard for them to maintain interest and enthusiasm in their work if they are totally dependent on their supervisor for stimulus, feedback, advice and support.

They do however have peers who are in the same position. Pairs or groups of students can exchange information, talk things through and share their experiences. They can give one another support which has the potential for being more varied, more relaxed, more sympathetic and more frequent than the support which their tutors are able to offer. There are also opportunities for students to make contact with other staff members and other researchers in the field.

•   **Joint tutorials**
    If you are supervising students who are working in the same area or who would for other reasons benefit from joint tutorials, suggest to them that they come to see you together, perhaps on a trial basis at first. (You could suggest this to your undergraduate students too.)

•   **Support groups**
    If you have 3 or more students, you can suggest that they meet as a support group. Encourage one of them to take on the job of organiser. You can help them yourself by offering to book a room on a regular

basis and perhaps attend their first meeting to answer any questions they may have. (You could offer this suggestion to your undergraduate students too.)

- **Postgraduate topic rooms**
  If your department is able to provide postgraduates with work space, consider grouping students by topic area rather than by year. In this way students working in different but related areas will be encouraged to discuss their work. A further advantage of this arrangement is that students in their first year, through discussions with students in their second and third years, will become aware of the different stages of a research degree.

- **Postgraduate mentors**
  Ask among your experienced postgraduate students for volunteers to act as mentors to beginning postgraduates. Point out to your new postgraduate students the advantages of having a mentor and ask them if they would like one. Put pairs of students in touch with each other.

- **Postgraduate staff-student liaison committee**
  Set up a staff-student liaison committee for postgraduates to consider any concerns they might have. The committee should meet between three and six times a year and the issues raised should be considered at academic staff meetings.

- **Contacts for postgraduates**
  Encourage postgraduate students to attend relevant conferences and interest group meetings, especially those specifically organised for research students. Attend conferences with them and introduce them to other researchers in the area.

- **Networking for postgraduates**
  Many interest groups now communicate via electronic mailing systems. Find out what is available in your area and make sure your postgraduates have access to these systems.

- **Social life**

  Neil Martin, writing in *The Psychologist*, February 1995, quotes the following among the replies received from postgraduate students who were asked what their advice would be to beginning PhD students:

  'When writing up don't become too isolated; force yourself to go out and relax and switch off from the PhD.'

  'Don't stop partying!'

  Your students could benefit from this advice.

(See also item 31, *Research students' discussion group*, and item 38, *Supervising students in groups*.)

Outside pressures 48

As well as being subject to the intrinsic stresses of university life, many students also have to contend with outside pressures, particularly financial hardship and relationship problems. As a supervisor, meeting regularly with your students on a one-to-one basis, you may well be the first person they turn to for help.

• **Financial hardship**
Financially it is hard being a student. Undergraduate grants have been severely reduced in value and postgraduate grants are now the exception rather than the rule. Students who do not have a supplementary source of income are obliged to put themselves in debt by taking out loans and overdrafts and need to spend valuable time in paid employment when they could be studying or even relaxing. Many students become anxious about their financial situation and exhausted with long working hours.

You can help your students by giving them information about any financial advice or other support which may be offered by your institution or Students' Union branch. You can also be flexible about arranging meetings with them to fit in whenever possible with their paid employment. Otherwise they could lose money or even their jobs.

• **Relationship problems**
Students may be in love or brokenhearted; they may have serious disagreements with their flat mates; they may have to deal with pressure of various kinds from their parents. Students in couples or families may also suffer from these problems and in addition have to renegotiate their home relationships to allow for the disruption and extra demands caused by student life.

You can help your students by showing that you are aware of the effect that relationship problems can have on their work and by giving them the opportunity to talk about their difficulties if they want to. Alternatively you may prefer to refer them to your student counselling service; they may prefer this too.

(See also item 28, *Supporting students emotionally.*)

Incompatibility 49

Students and supervisors are obliged to work together closely and often exclusively on a piece of work that is of crucial academic and personal importance to the student. Since it is beneficial if the supervisor has an interest in the specific area the student is studying, she is likely to have strong feelings and opinions about it too.

In this situation it is essential that student and supervisor work happily together. If they are incompatible, whether because of a personality clash or because of a fundamental disagreement about the project, the consequences are likely to be serious.

If as supervisor you have a compatibility problem with one of your students, you need to take responsibility for getting things sorted out. Many departments have a procedure which they follow, informally or formally. It usually looks something like this:

a The supervisor and the student try to resolve the problem themselves by talking it through. This requires each of them to speak openly and honestly about how he or she sees the other.

b If this fails, the supervisor and the student may feel they need to call in outside help. They may invite a colleague of one or both of them, or maybe a college counsellor, to help them talk it through.

c If both these methods fail, the student may need to be allocated a different supervisor.

It is a good idea to be aware of your own department's procedure. You may also need to formalise it and publicise it. Students find it reassuring to know from the start that there are ways of dealing with any clashes between them and their supervisors.

Blurred boundaries 50

The experience of supervision is very different from other lecturer-student encounters. This is due to the privacy of the relationship, the intensity of working one-to-one on a topic that both parties are enthusiastic about and the excitement of the highs and lows of the successes and difficulties of the work. In these circumstances it is easy for boundaries between supervisor and student to become blurred.

It is clearly appropriate as supervisor to support your students and care about their progress; it is not appropriate to allow yourself to get caught up emotionally in their anxiety or distress, or even their joy. You need to remember that the project, dissertation or thesis is the student's own and that over-involvement on your part is not merely misplaced but also potentially burdensome for the student and, more importantly, likely to cloud your professional judgment.

It is also wrong to allow sexual relationships to develop with students for whom you have responsibility as supervisor or examiner: in this situation, with its inevitable power disparity, the sexual relationship and the professional relationship would be likely to have a deleterious effect on each other. It would be difficult for justice to be done in the assessment of the student and impossible for justice to be seen to be done.

If you find yourself sexually involved with your student, then the proper course of action is to withdraw from the supervision role, inform your head of department of the circumstances and, if necessary, seek counselling help for yourself or the student.

If this is a case of True Love and you want to have a lasting relationship with the student you will need to wait until after he has been awarded the qualification.

'But they've done more than me!'   **51**

Although it may be possible to give students a general time-scale for projects, dissertations and theses (see item 24, *Reviewing progress*), in reality the detailed time-scale will vary from one student to another depending upon the nature of the subject matter and the research questions being asked. Some topics may require extensive preliminary work such as obtaining permission to work with particular populations, substances or materials, or building new equipment. Others may use readily available populations, substances or materials and existing equipment and therefore get under way quickly. In addition, different research questions may be best answered using different methodologies and this can cause further differences in time-scale. For example, in the social sciences or medical research, it is sometimes appropriate to collect data from the same people at several points over a period of time (a longitudinal study), whereas at other times it is more useful to carry out a series of studies involving different people each time who are seen only once (cross-sectional studies). As a result, even though two students may start at the same time and finish at the same time they may go through the intermediate stages at very different rates. They may also end up producing final reports which are qualitatively and quantitatively very different from each other. Thus, using the above example, one student may have collected extensive data from a few subjects, whereas the other student may have far less detailed data from a large number of subjects. If the students are colleagues this can be quite disconcerting for one or both of them.

It is important that as a supervisor you are sensitive to the different reasons why students may progress at different rates. Encourage students to draw up their own timetables and reassure individuals who are up to date in terms of their own programme. Discourage comparison with colleagues. If the practical work of one student is held up you will need to be supportive and do as much as you can to speed up the process. If two students are using very different methodologies (such as a longitudinal study and a series of cross-sectional studies) you need to anticipate future concerns by openly discussing the advantages and disadvantages of each methodology at the outset.

Cheating 52

Because they study independently, and are easily trusted by their supervisors, students working on projects, dissertations and theses have ample opportunity to cheat. As supervisor it is your responsibility to do what you can to prevent cheating and initiate an investigation of every case where you suspect it.

Cheating in this context is of three main types and each type requires action of a different kind on the part of the supervisor.

- **Plagiarism**

  Plagiarism, the unacknowledged use in assessed work of material from published sources, is a serious offence in higher education. As supervisor you need to familiarise yourself with the regulations on plagiarism in your institution and inform or remind your students of them. It is also a good idea to check that your supervisees know how to avoid committing plagiarism accidentally: advise them to make a scrupulous record of everything they read and keep full references, including page numbers, for all quotations (see item 15, *Basic advice for students*). In some cases it is advisable to warn them of the implications: in many institutions plagiarism carries a maximum penalty of failure. If there is a requirement that they include a declaration on the front page of their project, dissertation or thesis that it is all their own work, this should serve as a reminder to them.

  If you spot plagiarism at an early stage before the student's work is in its final form and it seems to be a case of careless note taking on the part of a student who is struggling to cope with large amounts of literature, it may be that a warning will be sufficient. However you should also keep a copy of the relevant passages, and your comments, for your records in case it occurs again in the final version.

  Normally a tutor who suspects her student of plagiarism is required to make a detailed case, which entails identifying the source of the plagiarised material and highlighting corresponding passages in the printed texts and the student's writing.

With the recent proliferation of possible source material, including the World Wide Web, some institutions have instituted a second type of plagiarism case in which the tutor presents circumstantial evidence which aims to demonstrate, for example, that the material is such that the student must have obtained it from an unacknowledged source, or that sections of the student's work are written in an uncharacteristic style.

Once the tutor has brought the case, the tutor and the student will then each be asked to make their case to a subcommittee of the examining board which will decide whether plagiarism has occurred, whether it was intentional and, if so, what the penalty is to be.

- **Outside help**
  This is a difficult one to define: you want your students to talk to their friends and relations about their dissertation or thesis and to get feedback but not to get someone else to write it for them. It is also a difficult one to demonstrate: there is no printed version for comparison as there is with plagiarism and your only reason for suspecting outside help may be a discrepancy between the quality of what the student writes and what he says in tutorials.

The best way to investigate a case of this kind is to test the student with a rigorous oral or written examination on his topic.

- **Fabricating data**
  Science and social science students who get tired of amassing data or who leave themselves insufficient time to produce all that they need or who simply want their data to be more impressive, may be tempted to fabricate some. As supervisor you are likely to spot this if you find inconsistencies in the data, achievements which would be impossible

in the time, connections which seem too neat, or other circumstantial evidence.

A case of this kind can best be dealt with by summoning the student, together with any of his assistants or subjects you can find, and confronting them with the circumstantial evidence.

Failure   53

So, you have followed all the advice in this book and tried out all the suggestions. And still your student fails. In that case, this is what you should do.

If, in spite of your best endeavours, your student fails, then it is probably because he is not capable - or not yet capable - of passing, either for academic or personal reasons. If in this situation you are tempted to blame yourself, forget it: it would not only be inappropriate but also likely to distract you from attending to your student's needs.

Students who fail need these things from their supervisor:

*   **Support**
    They need you to ask about and listen to their feelings: these may be feelings of inadequacy, disappointment, anger or resentment.

*   **Information**
    They need information about any possibilities of making good by rewriting and resubmitting their work.

*   **Encouragement**
    In the end they often need encouraging to face up to the reality of their situation and the new career and life direction which their failure entails.

.